ZEST for SUCCESS

A Quick Start Guide To Turning Your Dreams Into An Awesome Business

by Victoria Berry

COPYRIGHT

Zest for Success:

A Quick Start Guide To Turning Your Dreams Into An Awesome Business

By Victoria Berry

Print Edition

Copyright 2016 © Victoria Berry

ISBN: 978-1-326-73659-0

CONTENTS

ACKNOWLEDGEMENTS

My sincerest thanks go out to Charles Godfrey for his relentless drive in assisting me to finish this book. Charles, your forthright manner in questioning everything that was written has lead to this book being the best it could be.

To my Business Partners Tricia Bielby and Daren Cardow, this book has been a long-time dream of mine and a long time coming. Your understanding in the time taken by myself and Charles has been greatly appreciated.

Thank you also to my husband Daniel and kids, countless hours have been spent letting me just "get on with it". For letting me do my own thing and not interrupting – Thank You!

INTRODUCTION

WHY THIS BOOK?

There are numerous books on the market on how to start a business but in my journey as an accountant and start-up business owner, I have never found one that gives good, easy to understand advice that covers most of the information you need to know. So I decided to write my own.

As you can imagine, I get asked by existing and potential clients regularly what is required to start a successful business. These people are usually high on excitement about their new venture and extremely optimistic about the business world which they are about to venture into. The time and effort required to collate all the information that you need to know is enormous and extremely overwhelming. Furthermore, paying for it on a one on one basis is simply unachievable not to mention unaffordable!

Unfortunately, time and time again I have seen businesses fail, not from lack of effort by the owner but through lack of knowledge about how to start and run a successful business. It would be a great world if optimism equalled success but that simply is not the case.

Usually there are three reasons people start businesses:

- First is that they have a bright idea that they think has never been done before.

- Second is that they know their job and think they can do it better themselves and make more money doing so.

- Third is that their apprenticeship or their learning phase ceases and they either feel the need to go out on their own rather than continue with their current employer or don't have employment once their apprenticeship ceases.

This book is aimed at people who want to build a business that they can grow and ultimately sell to make a profit.

There are 100's of things to consider when starting a new business. This book will endeavour to go through some of the essential steps that you need to follow to eventually hit the ground running and to ensure that your business becomes viable in the shortest period possible.

The format of this book is in what I think is a logical order. You can either read it straight through or if there are areas of pressing need, feel free to jump from chapter to chapter. Within the chapters there are a combination of real life case studies taken from interviews with some of my top clients who have been in business over 20 years and some examples of fictional characters to explain the content another way. At the end of each chapter will be a list of "to do's" to help you identify the areas where you need to focus. Throughout each chapter are links to websites and documents that I believe will be useful as well. Please take the time to follow these links, some you will find useful, some you may not, in the end use the templates that you like.

Throughout the book I have included some case studies that are based on actual facts that I've seen over my accounting career. Obviously the names have been changed to protect the innocent but hopefully they bring to life some of the boring theory!

Lastly you will note that I often refer to "Xero" and "The Bookkeeper Hub". The reason for this is simple – The Bookkeeper Hub is owned by my accounting firm HBA Encompass and was established to provide small businesses with a simple online bookkeeping service that uses Xero as its "cloud based" bookkeeping and accounting programs. Whilst it may seem a blatant plug for both these systems, that is not the intention of this book, I am simply referring to products that I know and love and that I am sure will meet the needs of most small-businesses. Besides I needed to store the free templates somewhere so why not use my own website to do so! I have also included a chapter on the features and benefits of these products. There are many other excellent products out there but I consider Xero to be amongst the best.

Ultimately I wrote this book to assist anyone wanting to start a successful business. It is my intention that you will refer to it from time to time as you go along your journey as the basic concepts don't change over time. I look forward to hearing feedback from you as your business thrives and prospers.

CHAPTER 1

PLANNING

We've all heard the phrase before – "failing to plan is planning to fail" – well unfortunately it is true. When you are planning to start a business it is essential that you have a look at all the options that are available to you.

A friend of mine Gail Lockyer recently posted this relating to planning:

"I wish they taught every student the importance of goal setting and business plans. Great businesses don't just magically occur; they are the result of careful, strategic planning and realistic goal setting. Without a plan in place, the goal is just a dream. You need short term and long term goals but with some flexibility if something upsets the plan. Sometimes we need a Plan B. Make the goals achievable and measurable, the reward yourself or the team."

Banks and business coaches always talk about this plan that includes budgets and a marketing plan. This chapter aims to give you the basics and make it as simple as possible, so that you can understand where you need to go and to assess whether your business idea will work or not. There is no use going down a detailed business plan path if your idea doesn't have legs. There is more detailed information in following chapters that puts "meat on the bone" of the plan. This chapter is a basic guideline.

Foundations

Before looking at planning for your business, we need to step aside for a couple of minutes and think about the foundation of your business. Think of it like a house – you cannot start building walls until the foundations are laid.

Businesses need to be a combination of:

- Fundamentals or foundations – knowing how to run a business rather than being a good tradesman or technician. The ability to work on the business as well as in the business.

- Strategy – having a clear path to follow.

- Talent – the talent to show you can do whatever you do better than the others.

- Flair – the ability to be remarkable, exciting and memorable.

It is important to make sure that your business has these in the right proportions. Think of it as a pyramid:

Flair

Strategy & Talent

Fundamentals

Every decision you make during your planning stage needs to keep this pyramid in the back of your mind. You need to make sure that you have the fundamentals under control before you start adding flair (don't put the cart before the horse) or your business will look like this:

Let's look at what I mean by business fundamentals or foundation.

A business (like a house) built on flair and strategy but no fundamentals or foundation is doomed to fail.

It's just like the 3 little pigs:

The first little pig built his house out of flair – What a mansion, it looked good but underneath it was "made of straw".

The Second little pig built his house with flair, strategy and talent – a nice looking family home but underneath it was "timber".

The Third little pig had flair, strategy and talent but he also recognised the need to build his house with all the right Fundamentals – a solid family home with brick & tiles (think Sydney!)

Along came the big bad wolf (market/competitors) who blew and blew the houses in:

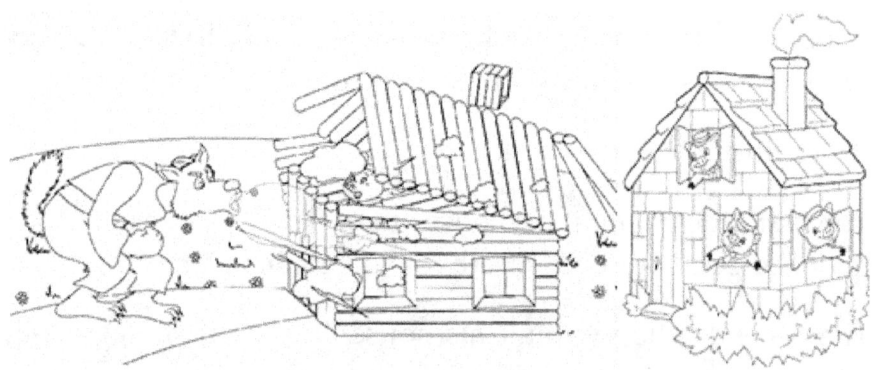

The First and Second pigs hadn't built their house with strong foundations and they were ruined.

The Third little pig sat drinking beer whilst the "cyclone" passed and then went out and helped the others clean up – he had the right foundations and building strength to survive the onslaught.

Product – What are you selling?

It is vitally important for you to be clear on what you are selling. Very often, we think that we are selling an item or a service but in reality, it is something completely different. Take a florist for example, it might seem that a florist is selling flowers but in reality, a florist is selling an emotional experience be it a wedding or a funeral. A restaurant does not just sell food – it sells an experience.

Once what you are selling is clear, the next step is to establish whether your product or service is satisfying a need and whether that need is sustainable in the long term. I am sure that you may have heard of the" hula-hoop" craze in the sixties. Establishing a business based solely on a short term market opportunity without prospects of diversifying into other products is generally not the way to go. That's not to say you won't cash in in the short term, but compare the number of "hoops" sold now to then, it's not a good long term business strategy.

Finally, will you be able to sell the product or service at a competitive price that will generate a satisfactory return on your investment? This will depend upon a number of factors that will include high volume – low margin products compared with more sophisticated and therefore more expensive products. It is vital that you understand where your product fits in this spectrum and that you are able to generate and maintain good margins on your product or service.

Target Market – Who are you selling to?

Before even starting on your business and your business plans, it is important to know if there is actually a market for your service or product. You need to know if your product or service has been done before, or if Your unique take on it is something different from what already exists in the market. In order to do this, you need to undertake some market research.

Most people stress out at the thought of market research because all they think about are the big research companies and the prices they charge. This is simply not the case. There are numerous websites that provide useful information on population demographics, competing products and much more. Some examples are industry websites, government census, libraries, trade magazines and business chambers to name but a few. See Appendix 2 – Useful Website Links for some links.

For most of us, "Google" is the first place to look. Think about what your business is going to do, and do some relatively simple searches to see if there are businesses in your area that are already offering your product or service and if your idea is different to these. Look for your major "point of difference" or "competitive advantage".

What is most important here is that you record your research so you can return to it later if needs be.

Another idea is to search for similar businesses in other towns or cities. Go and speak to them, let them know that you are looking at setting up and see if they have any words of advice or suggestions for you.

Example 1 – Mobile Hairdresser: Google "mobile hairdresser" and see how many of these exist and then do a few random clicks on the different businesses, preferably on page 1 of Google to see what they do. Is there something that is unique in how you are going to look at marketing your business. We talk more about Unique Service Positioning in our chapter on Marketing.

I cannot stress enough how important it is to get customer verification of your idea. It's one thing to ask friends and family if they think your idea is good but reality bites when you go out to the market with your idea. There are many ways to do this but the best way is to hit the streets. You need to find potential customers and test the market, not only on the product but also price, options and follow up.

Example 2 – Kids Toy Manufacturing: At a recent start up weekend, one team which was producing a children's toy hit the local parks to speak to parents, grandparents and the children themselves (with the parent's permission of course), they were there to test:

1. Did the parents think the children would like their toy?

2. What would the parents pay for such a toy?

3. Did the children like their toy?

The results were surprising – most parents didn't think the children would like the toy and wouldn't pay much for it, yet once the children got hold of the toy and started playing with it excitedly, the parents changed their mind and increased the price they would pay.

Word of Advice from John (Finance Broker since 2001): "Don't know it all, have an enquiring mind. Make sure you have someone that can give you critical yet objective advice and make sure you listen to both sides of the argument.

Having a product that people like and will be prepared to buy is not an automatic gateway to a successful business. You need to find out what your potential competitors are doing. Remember, as soon as they find out what you are doing, it's an odds-on bet that they will come out fighting with a comparable or lower-priced product. Once again, spend as much time as you need to understand your competitors, their business model, pricing and marketing strategies to ensure that you really do have a competitive advantage.

Unless you are convinced that you've got a business that is unique and has a significant competitive advantage, it will be back to the drawing board to see how you can tweak it to make it viable.

Operations

Now that you are confident that you have a product that will sell and you know who you are going to be selling that product to, you need to consider how and where you will operate. Items to consider include:

1. Premises

- How much floor space will you need?

- Where should you be located? Here you need to think about proximity to your target market and suppliers.

2. Equipment

- What equipment do you need?

- How much does it cost?

- Can it be rented or purchased on hire purchase? What would be the monthly instalments?

3. Staff

- Will you need to hire staff?

- What are their wages and associated costs?

4. Stock

- Will you need to carry stock? How much?

5. Cash or credit

- Will you be selling for cash or on credit?

- If on credit, you will need additional capital to fund your costs until they pay you.

Viability

The final step in your preliminary planning stage is to determine whether or not your business idea is viable, i.e. will you make sufficient profit to sustain your desired lifestyle in the medium to long term?

Budgets

Profit and Cash Flow budgets are one of the most vital things that you need to create for your business from day one. Even if numbers are not your thing, it is essential to know what your costs are going be, and compare them with an estimate of income, to see what effect that will have on your cash flow. While it is generally quite easy to estimate your costs, working out what your sales are going to be might be more difficult to ascertain. Equally important is to quantify not only your set up costs but also the costs of running for the first few months (and years) as sales slowly take off. You need to know if you have enough cash to operate until you are profitable.

There are absolutely oodles of budget templates out there on the World Wide Web. Different banks have their own templates if you are looking to obtain finance prior to starting your business. I suggest creating your own budget first, and then copying that into whichever template your bank of choice requests.

Different types of businesses need different types of budgets:

Fixed Costs Businesses – These are businesses that do not sell products but sell services which don't rely on extra inputs. This means they have fixed expenses such as rent, electricity, telephone. An example of this would be a graphic designer with one permanent employee who is not intending on employing another employee in the short term. Fixed Cost Businesses are relatively simple to budget for because their costs stay the same regardless of the changes in turnover.

Trading Businesses – These are business where costs change depending on the amount of sales. An example of this would be the sale of stubby coolers where the costs depend on the number sold or a business that sells services based on hours worked by employees.

If you have a trading business, then you need to calculate your "gross margin" or "margin" on sales which is arrived at by comparing the cost of sale with the selling price of the product and expressing the result as a percentage. It sounds technical but think of it this way – if I sell 1 stubby cooler for $6 and I know it costs me $4 to get it made then my cost of sales = 4 divided by 6 or 67% and the "gross margin" on each stubby cooler sold is $2 or 33%. Once you know this, you can predict your sales and let the budget automatically calculate the costs to produce those sales for you. Once you have established your "gross margin" on estimated sales, you can determine whether you will be making a profit after deducting administration and selling expenses and generating positive cash flow.

Manufacturing Businesses – If you intend on manufacturing the product, you will have to consider a wide range of manufacturing costs and overheads such as plant repairs and maintenance, operators' wages and "on costs" such as work place health and safety, factory consumables and power (electricity or gas).

If you have more than one type of product/service, you need to have different lines for the different types of product sales and different cost of sales so that you can see how much each product is contributing to your profitability. Changes in either the sales figures or margin % will affect your profitability and cash flow.

Profitability

Regardless of the business type, I always start with the expenses. It is usually quite easy to make an estimate of the business expenses that you will have. The templates referred to above have a list of the general business running costs. I have not included an estimate of the costs as these vary widely from business to business. A quick discussion with your Accountant or Bookkeeper may be able to point you in the right direction of what similar types of businesses are spending in these areas. If there is anything that is different about your business to other similar businesses, it is important that you include that expense item. An example of this would be hairdresser's who normally have very limited vehicle expenses that are generally only picking up stock, whereas if you are going to be a mobile hairdresser then you would have substantial vehicle expenses because you are going from client to client.

Once you feel that your expenses are correct, put in an estimate of your sales, apply your margin to the sales and then your budget should be populated.

When looking at pricing, yes look at your competitors but don't go into business with an undercut plan. By undercutting the prices of your competitors it sets you up on a quick path to failure, there is always someone out there with more resources than you who can sustain a long period of price cuts, your resources are limited.

The idea at this stage is to have a reasonable estimate of costs without going into the detail. That can come later. Once you have an estimate of the administration and selling costs, you can prepare a simple budget. I suggest that you budget for at least the next three years because under normal circumstances, it could take a year to eighteen months for sales to reach a level where the business starts becoming profitable.

Example 3: In our stubby cooler example above, we determined that the cost of the stubby cooler was $4 or 67% of the selling price of $6. The gross margin on sales is therefore 33%. Assuming that the total selling and administration expenses are $60000 for the year, the sales of at least $180000 will be required to break even before your personal drawings.

A: Selling and administration costs = $60000

B: Gross Margin on sales = 33%

C: Sales required to break even = $60000 ÷ 33% = $180000

If you believe that sales in the short to medium term of $180000pa are easily achievable, you can be fairly confident that your business idea will be profitable. If not, you have the following options:

1. Increase the price which in turn will improve the margin.

2. Reduce costs.

You could also review your target market and the sales assumptions to see if there is a realistic way you can increase the volume of sales.

In the final analysis, if the level of sales required to fund the costs is not reasonably easy to achieve in a year to 18 months, you should seriously reconsider whether or not you should proceed.

If you are confident that the business will be profitable, you need to set actual sales targets for the next three years. Applying the gross margin % to those sales will enable you to determine your estimated profit after Selling and Administration costs for each of those years.

	Year 1	Year 2	Year 3
Sales	120000	210000	240000
Gross Margin	40000	70000	80000
Selling and administration expenses	-60000	-60000	-60000
Net Profit (Loss)	-20000	10000	20000

So in the example given, the business will make a loss of $20000 in the first year but will be profitable from then on provided that the sales are achieved at the estimated margin. It follows that you can vary the sales and/or margin % to see what the effect will be on profitability.

Although, the business appears to be profitable, before making any decisions you need to consider your future cash flow and capital needs.

Will I have enough capital?

Capital is the amount of funds that you need to ensure the initial start-up of your business and ongoing operations. Capital can come from many sources:

- Cash injection by the owner(s);

- Bank Funding;

    o Overdraft;

    o Long Term Business Loan/Mortgage;

    o Equipment Finance (for vehicles or machinery);

    o Debtor Funding;

- Equity Partners;

- Loans from Friends/Family;

- Business Angels/Venture Capital.

These sources of funding are discussed further in Chapter 7 – Cash Flow Management. At this stage you need to be aware they exist but will need to explore them in more detail prior to proceeding.

The amount of capital that you need will be determined by your cash flow budget. Believe it or not, there is a difference between Profit and Cash Flow. A profit and loss statement shows on paper how much money your business has made and but the cash flow budget will show you where that money has gone, including your personal wages or drawings, capital expenditure and loan repayments.

Under the "operations" section above, I said that you should make a list of the capital equipment you will require. I also asked you to consider your stock levels and whether or not you will be supplying on credit because these items could have a significant effect on the amount of cash that will be required to fund the business.

Let's assume that:

1. You will require equipment at a cost of $10000.

2. You will need to hold at least one month's stock on hand.

3. 50% of your sales will be on credit with terms of 30-days settlement.

We can now prepare a cash flow statement for the business.

Example 4:

Sales	120000	210000	240000
Net Profit (Loss) -Example 2	-20000	10000	20000
Capital items	-10000		
Stock required	-6700	-5025	-1675
Debtors - 30 Days	-10000	-7500	-2500
Net Cash in (out)	-46700	-2525	15825
Cash Balance - previous year		-46700	-49225
Cash Balance - carried forward	-46700	-49225	-33400

So in this example, you will need start-up capital of $46700 in the first year increasing to $49225 in the second year but reducing in the third year as the profitability of the business improves.

I always suggest that you create a couple of budgets. By setting up a worst-case scenario, a best-case scenario and a middle-of-the-road scenario, it gives you a wider view of your business. At the end of the day, banks generally have their own opinions on how things will work, but if you have done the hard work on setting up these scenarios, you should be able to explain your logic. As long as your formulas work, it should be an easy process to change the inputs. This kind of thinking takes a bit to get used to, but once you can look at it and see where your money is going, you can really manage your business.

Real Life Examples – How Did They Fund It?

David (Finance Broker since 1983) – Existing Cash Savings. No budget because Excel wasn't invented yet, lived from week to week.

John (Finance Broker since 2001) – Bought into existing business using pay-out from old job & vendor finance from existing owner (David). Basic budgets, specifically for Sales as outgoings were stable. Now has both sales and income/expense budgets which are reviewed regularly.

Chris (Electrician since 1996) – Pay-out from previous employer & wife's earnings (bootstrapped). No budget.

Sandra (Day Hospital since 1998) – Bank Finance for both property & working capital. Budgets required by the bank for finance, regular reporting against actuals and budgets done by accountant.

Business Plans

Once you determined you have a market and have created your budget to prove that your business is viable, the next step is to create a business plan. In essence a business plan is a document that lists how you are going to run your business to achieve your business and personal objectives. A business plan is a living breathing document and it is something that should be reviewed regularly and updated as your vision of your business changes. It is not something to sit on your shelf, simply created because the bank requested one. On the upside, once you have created such a plan for yourself, you already have it to give to the bank or investors should they request one.

 **Real Life Examples – Use of Business Plan:**

Sandra (Day Hospital since 1998) – Detailed business plans were required by both the bank and our licencing authority. These plans had to be reviewed regularly for re-accreditation. This ensured we reviewed it regularly and noticed if we looked like deviating from our original direction. If we did deviate that was ok, we just had to update our plan, it was a living, breathing document.

John (Finance Broker since 2001) – We hadn't a detailed business plan when we started but undertook one several years later. That process made me really look at the things we did, how we did them and why we did them. It has lead to changes and improvements in the business since.

The basis for a business plan is really the chapters of this book. The things a good business plan will cover are:

1. Planning:

    a. Overview and Vision of Your Business;

    b. Your Unique Service Position (USP);

    c. Details of your product or Service; and

    d. SWOT Analysis (Strengths, Weaknesses, Opportunities & Threats).

2. Production:

    a. How the product or service will be developed and produced.

3. Marketing:

    a. An analysis of your market;

    b. Your competitive advantage; and

    c. Your marketing plan.

4. Structures – Your Business Structure Showing:

    a. Type of Structure to be used;

    b. Different responsibilities of different people? (Organisation Chart); and

    c. Organisation structure if applicable.

5. How Your Business will be Managed:

   a. Licencing Requirements;

   b. Processes and Procedures;

   c. Management Information Systems;

   d. Bookkeeping & Recordkeeping including debtor management;

   e. Premises;

   f. Staff; and

   g. Insurances.

6. Budgets

   a. Costs;

   b. Cash flows; and

   c. Profit and Loss.

7. Action Plans

There are numerous business plan templates available. Most governments, banks, and business organisations have free ones as well as numerous paid variations. The best thing you can do is to have a look at a few and see which suits you the best.

Verne Harnish's "One Page Plan" is a good way to work your end goal backwards into manageable chunks. For more information on this, go to www.gazelles.com to find out more.

Keep in mind here that if you are going for finance, it is often easier to create a business plan in a template that you like and can use and then recreate (copy & paste) your plan in the template that your bank offers. (Keep in mind here that banks have very strict guidelines and their people are not encouraged to think outside the square). A selection of business plan templates can be found at:

www.bookkeeperhub.com.au/templates/businessplans.

To Do:

1. **Check there is a market for your service or product.**

2. **Research costs and create your Cash Flow budget.**

3. **Find a Business Plan template you like, fill in the services & cash flow areas (the rest will come as we work through the rest of the chapters).**

CHAPTER 2

MARKETING

No matter what type of business you are in, whether it be sales of goods or services, online or offline or a bricks and mortar business, you need to understand what marketing is and how to get the biggest bang for your buck. This book is in no way a definitive answer to marketing, but hopefully it will give you some ideas that you can use to launch your business and get noticed. The important thing to remember in all marketing is consistency, meaning that all marketing you undertake is presented in the same style with the same branding. Ultimately you should end up with a marketing plan that fits in with your business plan. This doesn't need to be a massive document. A great one-page marketing plan can be found at www.1pmp.com, this has been created by Allan Dib who is also the author of "The 1-Page Marketing Plan", and it's quite a good read if you have time.

Understanding Your Target Market

Before you start throwing money at marketing, you need to know who you are selling to. They are the potential customers who are going to be buying your product. The market characteristics including the demographic (<u>for example, a single, female, middle-class, age 18 to 24, college educated</u>) and geographical area, and the needs of these potential customers will have a large impact on how you do your marketing.

Example 1: When selling a Porsche, your target market is likely to be men over 40 who have an income over $250,000 and have an ego to match the vehicle!

Example 2: When selling tie-dyed baby garments, your target market is likely to be a mother aged between 20 to 40 with little disposable income but who wants a product that will last.

Sometimes your target markets are not what you think they are. A great example was given to me recently by James Tuckerman of Australian Anthill fame:

I want you to picture a group of prospective customers and clients.

They are...

Men, aged 65+ (some are in their early 70s).

What do they look like?

What are their interests and hobbies?

Have you got the picture? Are you using your skills of imagination?

Have you formed an image in your head?

Now, what would you say if I told you I was thinking about the Rolling Stones?

It's not who you thought, is it? Sometimes you need to spend a little time "thinking outside the square" to determine your target market.

The point here is to make sure that you understand your target market because that determines how you get to them.

Market Capacity

Although you might offer an excellent product or service, you need to determine whether or not the market has the capacity to absorb a new product. This will require market research and a careful analysis of competitive products. You need to satisfy yourself that your product or service has one or more "unique selling points" or "competitive advantage" (discussed further below) or that other market factors such as a gap in geographical area warrant the risk of launching a new product into the market.

Understanding Your Competitors

It is vital for you to have an in-depth understanding of your competitors. What are their competitive advantages and how will they react to your product/service? How are they marketing their products? Having an informed knowledge of what they are doing will help in making your product or service stand out.

The 4 P's of Marketing

When marketing your business, there are four things that you need to think about and we're going to go into each of them in detail below. A lot has been written about the "4 P's of Marketing" which are Product, Price, Place and Promotion but here are mine:

1. Purpose: Your why. Why are you selling what you are selling? What is the reason behind your decision to go into business in the first place? You need to be able to explain to people why you have a passion for your business. If you want more information on your "why" Google Simon Sinek's "Start with Why" and watch a really interesting video.

2. UCP: Your Unique Champion's Position. This is similar to a USP or Unique Selling Proposition. A Unique Champions Position is slightly different however, as it is showing that you are the champion of what you do and not that you are just trying to sell. You need to clearly show people that you understand what their pain, fears, frustrations, hopes, dreams and desires are. Ideally what you are trying to do here is to identify and convince a section of the market that you have a product or service that eases their pains and frustrations or that will assist them to attain their dreams and desires. You need to sell the "experience" not the process.

3. Package: This is your unique solution to their problem. It is as much about the rewards of helping others as it is about your own personal rewards i.e. money. You need to show the purpose of what you are doing, the process of what you do and the payoff for your clients or customers. Ideally, the package offered should be a % split of 20% purpose (the "why"), 10-15% Process (the "How") and 65-70% about the payoff to the customer (the "Benefits" or "Experience"). It is important to only give a quick overview of what you do (no in-depth technical stuff) and focus on the outcome to the customer.

4. Promote: This is when you think about how to position and promote your package so that it will have the biggest impact in the long term. This is about building relationships with your customers.

I don't know if you have heard about the farming versus hunting analogy but it goes something like this: a hunter goes out and hunts once for his prize, i.e. a quick, short term return. A farmer on the other hand, finds some land, cuts down the trees, tills the soil, plants a crop, and is then able to harvest the crop on an ongoing basis.

If you translate both the hunter and farmer into business owner, you want to be able to reap the rewards of your efforts long into the future. You need to consider this analogy because you want to make sure that everything that you do is consistent in building long term relationships with your clients. By doing this, you will continue to sell to them over and over again.

Making the Most Out of Marketing

Following on, the 4P's of marketing is about consistency and getting the biggest bang for your buck. It is important here to think about matching your message to your market so that you are in front of mind when the people are ready to buy, whatever it is that you are selling. It was explained to me recently that selling is really professionally servicing other people's needs for a mutually beneficial gain. Big words but it means when somebody needs something and somebody can provide it, they will be willing to pay a fair price for it. A Win-Win; the customer receives the goods they want or need whilst the seller receives a fair price for providing it.

I am an accountant, not a marketing guru, what I am doing here is passing on some thoughts on the marketing of your business. I don't have a quick and easy one-off method to ensure your marketing success. You need to think about your target market and the best way to get your message to them and if necessary, seek professional advice.

Getting "Found"

It all comes down to getting "found" and that comes down to content. The idea is to convert strangers to suspects, then to prospects and ultimately to customers. Think of it this way:

Strangers – They don't know you and don't know why they might need you – you need to address their concerns and challenges before they will think that they need you.

Suspects – They know who you are but are not sure how you can help them – you need to show them what you can help them with.

Prospects – They know you but want more details – you need to demonstrate how you can help them achieve their goals better than your competitors.

Customers – They now know you and buy your product but you need to keep reminding them why they need your product. A good example of this is Coca Cola, one of the strongest brands in the world, yet they spend a fortune on advertising.

So how do you "get found"?

Leverage Technology

I'm sure you've heard of the "almighty" Google and SEO or "search engine optimisation". There is a constant stream of email marketers telling me that they can give me a ranking on Google page 1. Nobody except Google knows the exact algorithm to get you to page 1 (although they do provide some tips). There are hundreds if not thousands of companies that make money every day on helping business owners optimise their websites for Google. These people have put countless hours into their learning to be able to find the words and phrases that they believe your target market will be searching for. If you put in the right copy on your website, combined with AdWords campaigns hopefully you can increase your visibility. However, it will not guarantee you page 1.

If you want to plan your own SEO rather than paying for it, Google has lots of free information regarding how to do so, simply search "SEO help". Another place where Google can help is Google "AdWords", this will let you know what people are searching for and assist you with your planning.

Harness the Power of Audio Visual Presentations

Video has an extremely high ranking on Google presently so if your potential clients are not watching your videos, whose are they watching? Don't freak out thinking about videos, it doesn't have to be a picture of you perfectly made up talking to an audience, it may be simple screen capture of something that you are doing to be able to assist your clients to do something better with your product. Free video tutorials for your customer on your website or YouTube will not only make it easier for your customers to use your products, but also assists in your search engine optimisation. Don't forget to include your contact details with every video that you post. If you want to see some video's that have gone viral doing just that, search YouTube for "blenderguru". I'm not saying that you need to do silly things to go viral, more that you need videos to promote your business.

Give Something Away!

Another idea is to have a download of something free for your clients or potential clients to access from your website. Providing something that is useful to them will build a good relationship. Keep in mind here however, that you need to make sure there is an information capture process before they get access to the download. What this will do is build a database of potential customers that you can use in your ongoing marketing. When planning ongoing marketing, it is a great idea to think ahead – A systemised, automated process to keep in touch with customers and potential customers. What I mean here is a series of follow-up emails.

Examples of what you might provide free to convert your Strangers into Customers:

Strangers – A free fact sheet, map or poster on something relevant to your product.

Suspects – A checklist, roadmap or strategy on how to get past their own obstacles.

Prospects – Free product or trial period.

Customers – Loyalty card, bonus offers, ongoing low cost, high margin products and services such a virtual community or ongoing free educational material.

How Do You Get in Front of Strangers?

You need to touch base with them several times before they will become customers. Different numbers are bandied around by different academics ranging from 7 to 11!

Getting in touch but more importantly, connecting with Strangers is challenging to say the least.

The base plan to get them on the conversion map is:

Initial Contact

1. Touch base with them somehow, whether it be email, social media, website or other forms of paid advertising.

2. Offer an optional gift, a download of some type in return for their name and email.

    a. Use a landing page or email to thank them for subscribing and access to their gift.

    b. Make sure they can share the ability to download the gift with their social network (think Facebook, Twitter, LinkedIn).

3. Send follow up emails with a welcome, a promise and an offer of how you can help them. These are separate emails with separate useful content, not just a hard sell!

 **Case Study – Mechanic:**

Suppose I do a Google search for car mechanics in Brisbane and I click on the first one. A pretty standard website showing the contact details of the mechanic and some testimonials to show me how awesome they are but there is also a section to the side that says download our free eBook on changing a tyre. I've never changed a tyre before, and think this would be a good thing to know so I click on the download button. What happens then is a pop-up page comes up and asks me for my name and email address, there is also a little comment there about respecting privacy and spam rules but what they are essentially doing is collecting my information for future specials. One simple way to collect my information then I'm redirected to a special page on the website with the PDF document on the steps and pictures of how to change a tyre. I'm happy, I now know how to change a tyre. The business now has my details to be able to send out a link to other information documents that they may have. This might be set up as an automated process that comes out once a week for the next five weeks covering things such as checking water in radiator, filling up my windscreen wiper spray bottle, or whatever else mechanics can write about. It also allows them to send me a special offer that runs for the month of November in the form of a standard service for a small car for $130. What this does is keeps them front of mind for me. When I do need to have the mechanical work done on my car, either service or something major, I'm going to remember these guys because of the interesting information that came from them on a regular basis. As I said before you need to be front of mind when your customer is ready to buy.

Presentations

Presenting seminars or doing presentations to potential clients or investors can be an extremely nerve wracking experience. The payoff here is that if you can confidently explain your product on video, you should be able to sell it! Creating the perfect pitch is really about backing yourself and your product. You need to make sure that not only do you have the gift of the gab so to speak but also a strategy on how you are going to present to the appropriate people. Below are five things to keep in mind here when creating a presentation of any kind:

1. Confidence: Many people customers or investors want to see how you act under pressure. It is important to think about the potential questions they will have in advance, take a breath and speak with confidence about your service or product.

2. Know your product: It goes without saying that detailed knowledge of your business and your product is fundamental to creating a great presentation. You need to be able to talk with self-belief and detailed knowledge about whatever it is that you do. Keep in mind that it is not necessarily the technical detail of how you produce your product or service, but the outcome for your potential customers.

3. Demonstrate growth potential: Clients and investors need to know that your business has the ability to grow and to move forward. (Not to mention the ability to stay in business!) If you've done planning, and you know that you can create a viable business, demonstrating how you will get there should be a simple process.

4. Keep it simple: People generally don't want the technical ins and outs of exactly how you create a service or product. A great way to think about this is "the granny principle". If you can explain what you do in a way your Granny can understand, then generally your audience will understand it too. Everything that has been discussed above applies equally to any other kind of online presence you have, whether it be Facebook, LinkedIn, Google+, Twitter, Instagram or any of the other social media platforms. Ultimately it comes down to two things: Satisfying your customers' desires and needs.

5. Getting them back to your website: This not only allows you to collect their contact details for future marketing as described above but also to pay online if the facility is available.

Managing Your Website

Below is a summary of how to make your website and online marketing really work for you:

1. Consistency: Every time you send or post something, it should come out in the same way. This does not mean that you should email everything, it means that your branding should always be consistent across everything that you communicate. This includes logo, colours, style of writing, etc.

2. Matching your message with your market: Making sure that everything you write is presented in a way that your target market can understand and relate to.

3. Everything written must be about solving their problems: It is not about you it is about your customer.

4. Follow-up automation: Having a plan to collect data from potential customers and an automated system to keep in touch with them and keep you top of mind.

5. Landing pages: Your web designer will be able to assist you with this and many products such as WordPress allow the business owner to manage their webpage. This means that you can add pages behind the scenes to your website which link with your automated sequence. By having heaps of landing pages, you are able to measure the number of clicks through to a landing page, the number of downloads and the length of time that people stay on your site. This gives you an insight into what areas are working and which are not – allowing you to tweak your marketing quickly and effectively. Research also shows that viewers often go to your home page after they are finished on the landing page too.

Outsourcing

Unless your business is in marketing, there will always be people who can market your product or service better than you. What you need to consider here, is whether you are better off putting your limited resources (limited time) into learning about marketing for your business, or paying somebody else to assist you. There are a number of government programs that are free or at minimal cost that can assist you specifically in the areas such as SEO and Facebook marketing. Whilst these programs do give you valuable advice, what they really do well, is to provide you with enough information to be able to "sort the wheat from the chaff" so to speak when looking at hiring a professional marketing agency or person.

If you are adamant that you really want to keep your costs down and have control of your marketing, my suggestion is to engage the services of a professional marketing agency to work out a plan and a strategy for where you are going in your business. You should then be able to do the creation and the implementation of this plan yourself with some assistance from them or perhaps a part-time assistant.

Local vs. Offshore Outsourcing

There is an ongoing debate regarding local versus offshore outsourcing, and that is a decision you need to make for yourself. Keep in mind however that services such as www.upwork.com and www.fiverr.com have access to hundreds if not thousands of people who may be able to assist you for a small fee. Also keep in mind that a small fee does not always mean fantastic work and you may need to trial more than one of these outsourced contractors to get the standard you require. When looking at hiring such contractors, treat the hiring process the same as any other staff member. This means you need to look at examples of recent work they have done and recommendations they have been given by past clients.

I can go on for days here talking about marketing for your business and I'm not even a marketing professional. Take the time to do some research, let Google do some walking, and work out a strategy for moving forward. Once you have done this, ensure that you are consistent in your marketing messages and that you have a plan and process to ensure that there is adequate follow-up to your data gathering. The only advice I really have here is to keep reading and keep learning.

The basis of marketing doesn't vary much, however the methods, the terminology and the trends change constantly and it is important to keep up with them. A great idea here is find yourself a great marketing agency, subscribe to their download or newsletter, take advantage of the fact that they want to keep you front of mind for their sales and will continue to send you information that is valuable and marketing your business. Remember that the tools that they are using are valuable to you too.

To Do:

1. **Work through the 4 P's.**

2. **Plan your marketing.**

3. **Establish Automated Follow Ups.**

BUSINESS STRUCTURES

There are various types of business structure that can be set up to run your business. Some are cheap free and simple, others cost more to set up but have definite advantages in the long run. When looking at Business structures you need to consider:

- Initial Set-up cost;
- Asset Protection;
- Income Tax implications;
- Sale of Business Capital Gains Tax implications;
- Wind-up of the business implications;
- Ability to bring in new investors/partners; and
- Implications if something were to happen to one of your partners or shareholders.

Although we will discuss the different types of businesses below, it is recommended that you seek the advice of your accountant before choosing an entity structure.

No matter what type of structure you create, you still need to register for an Australian Business Number (ABN) and potentially a business name. It is common practice for banks to require the ABN number prior to opening a bank account and they will require the business name registration if you want that name on the documentation.

Sole Trader

Basically a Sole Trader is you. This is the quickest and easiest structure to set up. It is simply a matter of you deciding that you are going to go into business on your own, setting up an ABN or Australian Business Number, and starting to trade. If you want to trade in a different name to your own with a business name, then you need to register this with the Australian Securities Investment Commission (ASIC). The process for this is explained in Chapter 5 – Licencing & Fees. Keep in mind something as simple as "Bill Smith Electrical" needs a business name because it is not simply your own name.

The Pro's and Con's of being a Sole Trader are:

Pro's

- Quick & Easy to set up.

- You are the sole decision maker.

- Capital Gains can be reduced by 50% if you own an asset for greater than 12 months.

- Small Business CGT exemptions apply.

- No ongoing regulatory fees.

Con's

- Income tax rate is determined by your level of income and could be as high as 46.5%.
- No Asset Protection as it is in your name.

- You cannot bring in other investors without a change of structure.

- Business Name Registration is required.

Partnership

A Partnership is a common-law agreement between two people or entities (e.g. trusts or companies) or a combination of both.

A Partnership itself is free to create but because you never know when things may go pear-shaped, I highly recommend that you set up a Partnership Agreement from day one. Legal fees are required for this but the insurance that it provides you with in the event of a nasty split or the death of one party, far outweigh the costs involved.

Closure of Partnerships can create animosity between partners. A good Partnership Agreement will solve this problem. Another compelling reason to have a Partnership Agreement is to cover the situation where the Partnership looks to sell the business in the future. It is normal practice to require the general agreement of both partners. While this seems difficult, it is essential that partners act in the best interests of both themselves and the other partners at all times.

As with a Sole Trader, a business name registration is required through ASIC.

The Pro's and Con's of a Partnership are:

Pro's

- Free to set up.

- Capital Gains can be reduced by 50% if you own an asset for greater than 12 months.

- Small Business CGT exemptions apply.

- No ongoing regulatory fees.

Con's

- You should have a Partnership Agreement which is costly.

- You must have majority agreement on decision making.

- No Asset Protection if the partners are individuals.

- Both partners are jointly and severally liable for the actions of the other partner.

- Income tax rate is determined by the partner's level of income and could be as high as 46.5%.

- If you bring in new partners there is a capital gains event.

- Business Name Registration is required.

While Sole Trader or Partnership are the easiest to set up, they do not offer the same opportunities for reducing income tax rates and protecting the owner's assets.

To find out more about Asset Protection and Income Tax Rates affecting Sole Traders and Partnerships go to:

www.bookkeeperhub.com.au

Now let's look at other business structures that do offer asset protection and opportunities for tax savings.

Company (Proprietary Limited Company – Pty Ltd)

A Company is an entity that is set up in accordance with the Corporations Act and is a legal entity in its own right. A Company has shareholders who are the investors in the Company and directors who are responsible for the day-to-day running of the Company. It is possible to have a single shareholder and director Company however generally that is not recommended because should something happen to that shareholder/director it would make it extremely difficult for the Company to continue to trade and for the beneficiaries of that shareholder to maintain something of value.

It is important to remember that a Company is an entity in its own right as distinct from the shareholders. As such, it is able to buy and sell land, borrow, employ staff, and generally invest in any enterprise that it wishes.

The Pro's and Con's of a Company are:

Pro's

- Asset Protection for Shareholders.

- Small Business CGT exemptions apply.

- Tax rate 30% (28.5% for small business).

- Imputation Credits on Dividends.

- Business Name Registration not required.

Con's

- Initial set-up fee and ongoing regulatory fees.

- No 50% CGT exemption.

- If the Directors should issue Guarantees this removes Asset Protection.

- Limited flexibility with profit distributions.

Shareholders Agreement

As with Partnerships, if you are creating a Company with a business partner (wife or family members included), I strongly recommend that you create a Shareholders Agreement at the time of this Company set up. This agreement will regulate the actions of each individual shareholder and in addition, provides instructions on inter-alia:

- Payment of dividends;

- Remuneration;

- Appointment of shareholder directors and their roles and responsibilities;

- Sale of shares; and

- Monetary and other matters to consider in the event of a winding up of the Company or a falling out between shareholders.

Set up and Regulatory Fees

The costs of setting up a company will vary depending on the complexity and the service provider but would typically start at $1200.

More details on set up including company name and regulatory fees can be found at:

www.bookkeeperhub.com.au

Trusts

There are various types of trust structures but the most commonly used types of trust structures are family or discretionary trusts. Before discussing the various types of trusts and their role in tax planning and profit distribution, there are a few terms that you need to know:

Settlor – person who gives the trustee a nominal amount, say $10, to invest on behalf of the beneficiary (usually your accountant or lawyer).

Trustee – person who is responsible for looking after the investment on behalf of the beneficiaries.

Beneficiary – person or entity that is entitled to a share of the profit of the trust (the Business Owner is usually the Primary Beneficiary with family members being secondary beneficiaries).

Appointer – person who has the ability to change or remove trustees (generally the Business Owner/Primary Beneficiary).

The basic logic behind a trust is that the Settlor gives the Trust (trustee) money (usually a nominal amount of $10) to create the trust. The Business Owner or Primary Beneficiary loans the trust sufficient funds to establish the business and to provide it with start-up working capital. The trustee is responsible for investing money that the trust receives from the Settlor and Primary Trustee on the behalf of the all beneficiaries.

Types of Trusts

There are three main reasons for setting up a trust:

1. Tax savings;

CHAPTER 3 – BUSINESS STRUCTURES

2. Asset Protection; and

3. The ability to own assets from one generation to the next.

These factors are discussed more fully at:

www.bookkeeperhub.com.au

The most widely used trust is the **family or discretionary trust** so let's look at that first.

A Family Trust is generally set up to create wealth for the beneficiaries of this trust. The beneficiaries of the trusts are generally related to the business owner or Primary Beneficiary. This means that the wife, children, grandchildren, parents, grandparents, aunts and uncles of the Primary Beneficiary are generally able to receive distributions from this trust. Often companies within the family group can receive distributions from trusts as well (depending on the deed). The trustee is responsible for deciding who within the family group receives a distribution. This means that the trustee needs to look at the profits of the trust prior to 30 June and determine who that profit is to go to. Both Family Trusts and Discretionary Trusts are generally discretionary in nature, the only real difference being in that one is called Discretionary and the other called Family.

Say the Smith Family Trust was set up with the following information:

Settlor – Mr Accountant

Settlement Sum – $10

Trustee – Smith Enterprises Pty Ltd

Primary Beneficiaries: Bill & Mary Smith

This means that Smith Enterprises is to invest the $10 for the good of Bill & Mary Smith. In reality Bill & Mary Smith wanted to buy the local take-away business and contributed $150,000 for the purchase. At the end of the year the business had made a profit of $50,000. The Trustee, Smith Enterprises must decide prior to 30 June who to allocate this to. As Bill was working at the Council, they decided to allocate $400 to each of the kids and the Balance to Mary.

The Pro's and Con's of a Family Trust are:

Pro's

- Flexibility to distribute profits;

- Asset Protection;

- Tax rate depends on each beneficiary;

- No ongoing regulatory fees (unless you have a company as trustee);

- All CGT Rules apply providing beneficiary is a natural person; and

- Ownership of assets through generations.

Con's

- Distribution needs to be decided prior to 30 June each year;

- Cannot bring in investors other than immediate family;

- Financial Statements must be prepared; and

- Business Name Registration is required.

Unit Trusts or Fixed Trusts

Unit Trusts or Fixed Trusts are a bit like a Company and are usually set up when businesses are being established with partners who are not family members. The main difference from other trusts is that individual unit holders have a fixed entitlement to the trust profit. The trustee is generally unable to change this distribution from beneficiary to beneficiary. Otherwise, all trusts operate in the same way and the same pro's and con's apply.

There are no further ongoing fees for trusts other than preparation of financials and tax returns, however if the trust does have a business name then there will be an annual fee for this service, this will be discussed further in licencing and registration.

Summary:

Entity	Sole Trader	Partnership	Company	Trust
Annual tax return	Yes	Yes	Yes	Yes
Financial statements required	Recommended	Recommended	Yes	Yes
CGT exemptions	Yes	Yes	Limited	Yes
Marginal tax rate	Individual	Individual partner	30% (28.5%)	Individual beneficiaries
Ongoing registration fees	No	No	Yes ASIC	No
Limited liability	No	No	Yes (2)	Yes (2)
Setup fees	$0	$0 (1)	Yes	Yes
Ease of setup	10	7	8	5

(1) Partnerships technically have no setup fees however a partnership agreement is suggested.

(2) Whilst companies and trusts have limited liability, should directors or trustees give personal guarantees then there may be a liability on them individually. Also note that where companies trade insolvent, directors may be liable. New ATO regulations regarding outstanding PAYG, GST, and superannuation may also be attached to individual directors or trustees.

To Do:

Discuss with your accountant the best entity structure for your business.

CHAPTER 4

MARKETING AND TECHNOLOGY

Our previous chapter on Marketing talked about understanding our target market, your competitors, the 4 P's of marketing and briefly touched on leveraging technology to achieve your marketing goals. This chapter is to give you more insight into the ways that technology can help you. As a director of 3 separate yet similar business, I have been directly involved in not only marketing strategies but also the implementation of Technology for cash-strapped start-ups. The goal here is to pass on some of what I have learned to assist you in ramping up as quickly as possible.

In a nutshell, the aim of Technology is to get your marketing message in front of as many people as quickly and regularly as possible with the least labour input and the lowest cost. This is not to say that we are trying to sell at all times and in the Social Media scene, constant selling will only turn off potential customers.

Let's go through some of the technology available and how it can help, followed by a suggested structure that may assist you.

Social Media

Social Media is one of the quickest and cheapest ways to get your branding out to people. Social Media is available on both free and paid platforms. <u>The golden rule with all Social Media is to never post (say) anything that you wouldn't say to someone face to face!</u> If someone upsets you, sleep on it before posting a nasty reply. Below is a summary of the Social Media Platforms that I am most comfortable with:

1. Facebook

Facebook is by far the most common Social Media Platform. Most of us use it to connect with friends and family but it can also be used as a business tool.

    a. *Groups* – One of the most common ways to promote yourself is to look for groups with common interests. These groups can be public (meaning anyone can join/post) or private (meaning you must be accepted by the administrator or moderator before you can post). There are groups on nearly everything you can imagine. The best way to achieve traction within a group is to give freely. Of course you can use them to ask any type of related question but in providing answers you show yourself as knowledgeable in your field. This means that when people are ready to buy, you are not only top of mind but also top of mind to refer to family and friends. Be mindful that different groups have different rules so always check the rules before posting, i.e. a Classifieds Group is there for selling of goods, not for posting general updates on lost dogs. If there isn't a group that suits your niche, you can always start one.

b. *Ads* – Facebook allows you to create targeted ads to reach out to different target audiences so you can structure your marketing message directly to those you want to speak to. You can target location (country, region, postcode or the area around your business) and demographics (age, gender, interests and language). Think back to the target market comments in Chapter 2 regarding the middle aged men, and imagine being able to promote your golf packages to men over 50 specifically who like golf. There are also opportunities to create custom audiences and lookalike audiences which lets you find the people who are similar to your best customers – quite scary really. Naturally they are mobile friendly by default. Facebook backs it all up with statistics so you can see which ads are working and which ones are not. You can choose the budget and the audience and you can edit or stop your budget at any time. The best way to find out more is to look at Facebook's help: www.facebook.com/business

2. LinkedIn

LinkedIn is a social networking site designed specifically for the business community. The goal of the site is to allow registered members to establish and document networks of people they know and trust professionally (source: Wikipedia). Unlike Facebook or Twitter, there must be an existing relationship between members to make a "connection", although this can be as simple as another shared connection. While most "shares" on Facebook appear to be photos and quotes, LinkedIn shares are usually business information that members have either created or found elsewhere and shared. LinkedIn is also an unashamed promotion of what you have achieved and the ability to promote your contacts for their achievements.

a. *Groups* – Like Facebook, LinkedIn has groups. The same logic applies here, i.e. "giving to receive" however LinkedIn is more open to promotion of your business within these groups.

b. *Advertising* – LinkedIn also has an advertising function. You are able to select your audience by job title, job function, industry, geography, age, gender, company name, company size or LinkedIn group. It is charged by "pay per click" and you have control over the maximum number of clicks you will pay for.

www.linkedin.com/advertising has all the detail on how to actually create an ad and the costs involved.

c. *Premium* – LinkedIn Premium is a paid subscription which will allow you greater ability to link with the right prospects. It has lead searches that allow you to target your contacts in a similar fashion to ads but you can approach them directly to connect and at the same time, unlock up to 25 profiles per month to get more information on them before you approach them. An interesting feature of Premium is that you can see who has viewed your profile in the last 90 days and reach out to them or save them as leads.

You can also reach prospects directly with "InMail" even if you don't have their email address, allowing you to send up to 30 messages per month rather than cold calling. Premium can integrate with the online CRM system Salesforce too. www.premium.linkedin.com

3. Twitter

Twitter is something we see almost nightly on various reality TV shows but it can also be used for business as well. A post on Twitter is called a tweet (it's logo looks like a bird). It is an expression of a moment or an idea about what is going on around you. The idea is that a tweet can be shared in real time and it may contain text (up to 140 characters), photos or videos. This means that the opportunities are endless. Sending a tweet is only useful however if people "re-tweet" meaning they send it on because they think it is interesting. People can add their own comments to your tweet before re-tweeting. A Hashtag # allows other people interested in your tweet to follow the story to see what is going on, think #Worldcup and the numerous updates about the rugby that will come from all over the world. It has been proven that tweets with pictures or videos have more re-tweets than those that containing just comments. Your username is called @username – think @bookkeeperhub. Twitter has an advertising component as well and the three types of advertising are quite different:

a. *Twitter Promoted Tweets* – Those that you have already tweeted (posted) that you wish to promote. These ads can be targeted by interests, targets, gender, device, geography and similarity to other followers. The costs of these vary between $0.50-$2.00 per click, depending on your targeting. An average is $1.35.

b. *Twitter Promoted Accounts* – Offers you the ability to promote your account to potential followers – like LinkedIn's suggested contacts. You can target by interest, geography and gender. Pricing depends on your targeting but generally you pay between $2.50-$4.00 per follower.

c. *Twitter Promoted Trends* – Provide a massive exposure for a short period of time – guaranteeing your promotion in the trends of the day. Expect to pay $200,000 per day so most likely out of the range of small business!

One of the additional benefits to advertising on Twitter is that you gain access to analytics to everything you post on Twitter, not just your paid posts. This provides great insights into which tweets perform best and insights about your followers. You also have more chance of gaining a verified account.

4. Google+

Google+ is one of the Apps created by Google that integrates with all things Google. This means it starts with your base Google Account and it integrates with the Social Media, Blogs, YouTube and Google Hangouts. It is possibly the most interactive of all the Social Media Sites due to its interconnectivity. Google+ doesn't have lists or friends, it has Circles which are based on your individual interests.

Communities are Google+ groups, which allows you to keep your connection with these people separate from your newsfeed meaning that you don't have to see photos of their babies, only posts that are relevant to the community. You can have individual settings on each community to control the type of content you want to receive. Given that Google controls the Play Store (Android istore), it has lots of interactions with Android devices.

a. *Google Hangouts* – A webcast program which can be used for teaching, business presentations, podcasts, etc. It can be linked directly to YouTube to provide watching afterwards.

b. *Ads* – Google+ doesn't have ads. Google users will spend enough time in search to utilise the normal Google AdWords which are discussed later in this chapter. Using Google+ as your social site does however increase your rankings in Google searches.

5. Pinterest

Pinterest is a visual bookmarking tool that allows you to discover and save creative ideas. It is valuable too, basically a massive photo and quote sharing site. Like other social media platforms, you can follow other users if you find their content relevant and their content will show up in your feed. If you see something in your feed, or search for it, then you can pin it to a board to save for yourself for later. The benefits here are that if your board is public, your followers can see what interests you and as the pins always point back to where the pin came from so the history of the creator is never lost. This means if you create content (think a homeware store) and someone pins it, when they are ready to buy they know where it came from and can contact you. It needs to be noted here that whatever you pin needs to be visual – pictures, pictures, pictures.

    a. *Promoted Pins* – Like other social media sites you can promote a pin which makes them appear in the most relevant places. You can target your audience and pay per click. Pinterest does have rules regarding their advertising: https://about.pintrest.com/en/advertising-rules which seem pretty straight forward to maintaining an enjoyable experience for users.

6. Instagram

Instagram is an online mobile photo-sharing, video-sharing and social networking service that allows users to take pictures and videos and share them on a number of social media platforms such as Facebook & Twitter. It probably goes without saying that this too is a visual platform and you need to have great content. The point of Instagram is to make connections with people that see the world in interesting ways, i.e. to connect with people that like the same things as you do or what you are promoting. Instagram has 3 types of ads:

    a. *Image Ads* – These simply promote your photo as a sponsored photo with a call to action button linking back to your website and the ability to install mobile apps too.

b. *Video Ads* – These offer the same features as image ads but you can share videos of up to 30 seconds long and in landscape format. A call to action button can link back to your website or app download.

c. *Carousel Ads* – A collection of ads rotating across your screen – People can swipe to see additional images and the call to action button takes them back to your website (a collection of 2 or more image ads).

Interestingly, now that Instagram is owned by Facebook, you can place your ads through the Facebook Power Editor and manage both types of ads from the one place.

7. YouTube

YouTube is the second biggest search engine of them all, surpassed only by its parent Google. Anything and everything is available on YouTube. Video is the most watched content in the world. YouTube links with all other social media platforms. The bottom line is that if you create content, you should add it to YouTube and promote it on all your other social media. Given that YouTube is owned by Google, having content on YouTube with good tagging will rank well in Google Search.

1. *YouTube Ads* – Different to other types of advertising, they are videos placed to appear in front of other people's videos. Apart from that they are similar to other social media in that they allow you to target by age, gender, location interests and more. They also work on a pay per click model and if the watcher skips the ad you

don't pay. To be honest I haven't had any experience with YouTube advertising, you can read all about it:

www.youtube.com/yt/advertise

So How Do I Manage It All?

We have talked about 7 types of social media and there are many more that we haven't covered. Trying to juggle all of your social media accounts can be tricky and time consuming. If you are anything like me, open Facebook and boom, there goes half an hour checking out what everyone else is doing. Luckily there are lots of tools available to manage your accounts in one place, allowing you to scan what is going on, post across multiple accounts & schedule posts for times that are going to suit your audience. They all target different platforms and have different capabilities. Below is a table that attempts to summarise it all for you: *Prices correct at time of writing:

Table (opposite) references:

1. 17% cheaper annually.
2. Up to 12 profiles.
3. Plus 31 more networks!

Tool	Free	Paid	Schedule	Insights	Niche	Networks
Hootsuite	Y	$10.99	Y	Y		[3]Facebook, Twitter, LinkedIn, Google+, Pinterest, YouTube
SocialOomph	Y	Y	Y		Autofollow	Facebook, Twitter, LinkedIn, Plurk & Blog
Tweepi		[1]$7.49-$14.99			Cleanup tool, reciprocate by following	Twitter
Spreadfast					Reach of posts	Facebook, Twitter, YouTube, Flickr
Buffer		[2]$10	Y	Y		Facebook, Twitter, LinkedIn, Google+
Sprout Social		$39 - $99	Y	Y		Feedly, Facebook, Twitter, Google+, LinkedIn
Everypost	Y				Twitter text shortener	Facebook, Twitter, Google+, Pinterest, LinkedIn
Bitly	Y			Y	Shortens post links	Facebook, Twitter
Social Flow		$99			Relevance	Facebook, Twitter
Crowdbooster		$9		Y		Facebook, Twitter

I use Hootsuite and love it. Keep in mind however that whilst tying all your social media together is a great time-saver, not every message is right for sending to all of your networks at once. You may need to think about which network you want to post to and only schedule posts to them individually rather than a bulk post. Remember that social media is great for special promotions and branding but the real test is in driving them back to your website.

Email Campaigns

Email is one of the easiest ways to get a message to someone. If used effectively, an email campaign can be a great way to promote products and grow your data base of leads and prospects. Funnily enough, a good email campaign is more than just email and uses social media and web technologies to deliver great content and calls to action.

Before you even think about creating an email campaign, you need emails. Simple? Australia has very strict anti-spamming laws and since their inception, it's extremely hard to purchase client lists that are current and have the required "opt-in" from the contacts. Each person needs to sign up to your list for you to be able to send them unsolicited emails. I did however read recently that it is ok to send unsolicited emails to businesses providing the email is directly related to their business. The example given was emailing a plumber a brochure on plumbing supplies. The anti-spam laws still do create a problem for a start-up business as you have no-one to send your email campaign to. For this reason, we have put this section below social media because social media is how you can create this list. More on this later.

Assuming you have a list of emails where people have signed up for you to send content, the next question is how are you going to send it? Most email providers will block bulk emails to groups over 50 as they determine it to be spam. This means you need to have a program that allows you to create content and deliver it to your prospects in an easy and efficient way. Spending your days sending 5 emails at a time is both costly and a waste of your time in this day and age. There are numerous bulk email programs available and we use MailChimp but other common ones in Australia are Aweber, and CampaignMonitor. When choosing a service, you need to look at both your usage and the number of addresses you want to add. I'll talk about MailChimp as we move forward but I'm sure the logic is all the same.

It's essential when sending out a mail campaign that you work out exactly what you are aiming for and how you are going to do it before you even start. Studies have shown that the average prospect needs 7 touches before they buy from you. If you are anything like me, you get oodles of emails each day and unless there is a headline that grabs you "Delete" is the button of choice. It is essential to have an attention catching headline and good content followed by a call to action. Don't expect people to buy on the first email – you don't get married on a first date, you need to court your audience. Generally, this is done in the traditional manner – gifts. These needn't be of massive monetary value but more-so, items that are valuable to the potential lead and valuable to the client. Examples here might be, a Template or Flow Chart. We talked about this in more detail in the previous chapter.

Most importantly, once you have your email template set up – send one to yourself to test it before you let loose on the unsuspecting public – there is nothing worse than a poorly formatted email to make the potential customer delete your emails in the future.

Websites

Websites are more than electronic brochures – in many cases they are your potential customer's first glimpse into your business. Website set up costs vary from Free to Tens of Thousands of Dollars. Whilst it is important to get the basics right, sometimes it's best to start small and grow the features as your business develops.

Regardless of how you set up your website, where possible make sure that the domain name (web address) of your site is your business name, i.e. www.bookkeeperhub.com.au. There are usually a few basic pages on your website: Home, Services, About us and Contact. Web developers charge per page so make sure you cover what you need to but don't go overboard. Where possible get instruction from your developer so that you can edit the content and add pages yourself. Make sure you use a well-known website program so that if you need to part ways with your developer, you can take the site with you and others can update and manage it if needed. One of the most common website development packages is WordPress.

Websites often have hidden pages called landing pages that don't show on your main pages or directory. These are used for specific purposes such as a link to a current promotion. Generally, there is no limit to the number of landing pages you can have and learning how to set them up is essential so we are going to go into more detail on them shortly.

If you are unable to get a site up and running quickly, it may be possible to use a program such as Leadpages to create landing pages to go with your marketing and assist in the use of technology, we will cover this shortly too.

Search Engine Optimisation (SEO)

SEO is the system of making sure your website is open and accessible to the Googlebots who go around the internet cataloguing websites for Google. By using SEO, you can increase the numbers of people to your website by obtaining a high ranking placement in the results pages of a Search Engine such as Google or Bing. The actual techniques of SEO would take a whole book in itself but what is important to note here is that no-one can guarantee you front page of Google because no-one knows their exact algorithms. Careful placement of words and "Meta-Tags" can assist in your ranking but it takes time, effort and knowledge. SEO Experts can assist with this placement and "Tagging".

Ultimately "content is king". If you have content that is both engaging and useful with a smattering of useful keywords, then the chances are that you will rank with the Googlebots. The content that they will look at includes the text, titles and descriptions of pictures. They also look at the look of the site, how easy it is to navigate around and the speed at which it loads. Note that if you duplicate other people's content you will be penalised so always write your own content, never cut and paste.

So how does it all link together?

Aha, that is the magic question. The answer is "it depends". It depends on how you want to manage your marketing – are you going to do it yourself, automating as much as possible or outsource it?

My 10 steps to create a Social Media and Email Marketing Presence:

1. Create your Social Media Profiles – Always complete your profiles in full regardless of platform.

2. Search for Groups that match your target client and join (or ask to join).

3. Search for individuals that you want to connect with (where possible – this differs with each platform).

4. Use Hootsuite to Monitor your platforms and give answers and feedback where necessary.

5. Ensure you have great content to deliver a system of gifts to entice prospective customers – this can be fact sheets, flow charts, white papers, videos.

6. Design a marketing campaign – The sequence in which this content is to be delivered.

7. Create the designed landing pages for each content – Make sure that the first one in sequence has a requirement for subscribers to add their name and email address so you can keep it to direct the information to them personally for the rest of the sequence.

8. Automate the sequence and delivery of the content.

9. Make sure your last few content downloads have calls to action so that they are able to buy your product or service.

10. Go back to number 2 and continue to grow both your social presence and email list to continue to market your products and services.

Example: Let's go back to our mechanic example from Chapter 2 – Marketing. Assume he's created his social media presence:

1. His target market is busy female professionals.

2. He creates a program of different fact sheets about car care including links to YouTube Videos on how to do what is in the fact sheet, i.e. change a tyre.

3. He creates a call to action "See the easiest way to change a tyre without getting your hands dirty".

4. He doesn't know much about his website so he subscribes to Leadpages to create the landing page for the first interaction.

5. He takes out Facebook & LinkedIn Ads targeting Females within a 10km radius of his workshop who work as Real Estate Agents, Accountants & Lawyers with his call to action, linking to his Leadpages page.

6. He also posts his call to action in his other regular social media pages with a link to the Leadpages page.

7. This page has a call to action "See the easiest way to change a tyre without getting your hands dirty" which when clicked on, requests the prospect to put in their First Name, Suburb and email address. This then takes them to the link to watch the video.

8. Leadpages links to his MailChimp and puts the prospect into a specific campaign called "Lady Drivers October 2016".

9. MailChimp then sends out the rest of the content on a weekly basis to his audience for 5 weeks.

10. The final email in the MailChimp sequence ends with a Call to Action "Book now to save $50 on a pre-Christmas Inspection – Go on holidays knowing your car will get you there and back".

11. In January he starts another campaign to another target audience.

12. He now has a growing MailChimp list to send other ongoing specials or information to encourage more purchases.

Note: Using automation, our mechanic can create the same campaigns to different target audiences at the same time with different calls to actions or triggers to get their attention. It can be endlessly repeated with no extra effort.

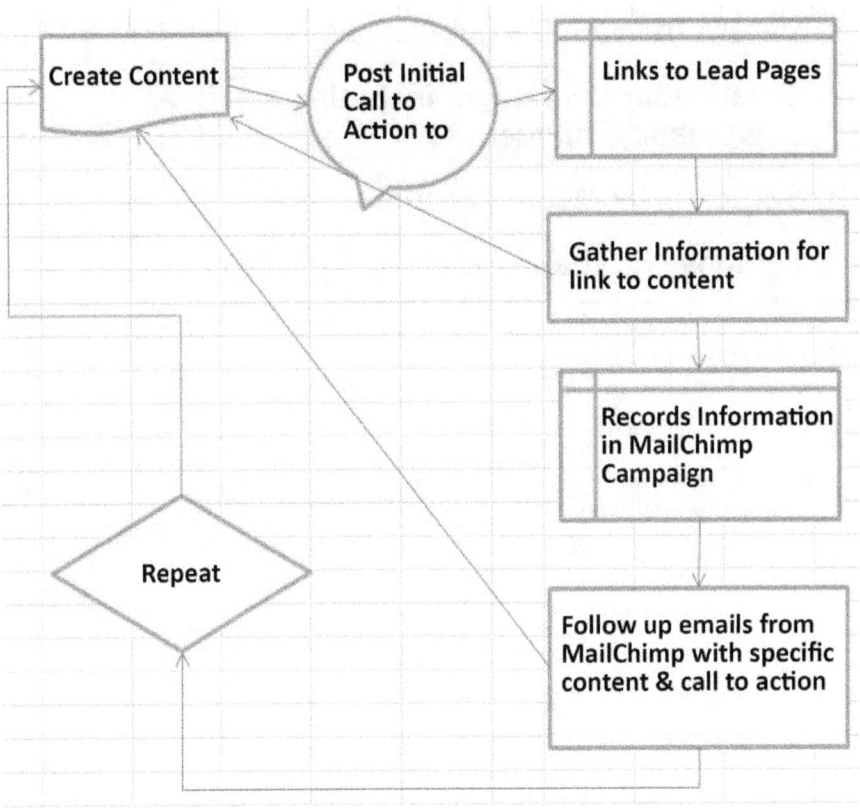

To Do:

1. Determine your Target Market.

2. Create your Campaign, including emails, downloads & sequences.

3. Setup Social Media Accounts.

4. Let loose on the world.

CHAPTER 5

LICENCING AND FEES

Whilst it is relatively easy to create a business structure, it is important to think about the various licenses and registrations that you may need to start and run your business.

Business Names

If you operate as a Sole Trader and you want to have a business name registered that is different from your own name, it is essential to make sure that the business name that you require is actually available. Similarly, if you decide to create a Company you must check that your preferred company name is available. Trusts can be registered with the same name as any other trust that is currently registered. It is therefore important that a trust has a business name registration so that it is distinguished from other trusts. It is also advisable for a Trust to have a company that is the Trustee in the business name that you want. An example of this would be ABC Earthmoving Pty Ltd ATF the Smith Family Trust, most people would associate the business as ABC Earthmoving.

To check a business name's availability, go to www.asic.gov.au and search for the business name of your choice. If your business name is different to those listed, then you can easily register the business name by following the prompts. If the name that you want is similar to other names on the list on the register, then try combinations of other spellings or see if there is something different that you can add to your registration to make different to the ones that are listed.

Example: You want to register your business name as brothers Plumbing. When searching the register, you find there is already a Brothers Plumbing Pty Ltd. If you change your name to Brothers Plumbing (Qld) Pty Ltd then it is ok to register it.

A business registration can have either an annual or a three-year registration fee. The good news with this is that it makes it harder for people to change their business into the name that you already have. However, if you trade under a business name that is currently in use and the owner of the business name finds out about this, you do open yourself to massive legal liability.

If you intend using a company, you need to get your accountant to set it up for you and once it has been incorporated then the business name is automatically taken without ongoing fees.

Industry Licences

There are other licenses that you may need to think about depending on the type of business that you intend operating in. For example, in Queensland there are industry bodies such as the Queensland Building & Construction Commission (QBCC) for builders or tradespeople who need to be registered with the QBCC www.qbcc.qld.gov.au. This is a government body that regulates the building industry and there are similar bodies in other states. Another example of an industry licence is Bookkeepers who are required to register as BAS Agents.

There may be training required in order to meet these industry body qualifications or government qualifications. If you have these qualifications, you need to have the necessary documentation available to ensure that your registration goes through smoothly. If you do not have the qualifications, then you must ensure that you obtain them as soon as possible because you will not be able to start your business without the approved training.

Other Fees & Licences

Other licences or registrations may include council licences & fees. Depending on the industry you are going into, it is advisable that you contact your local council to see if there are licences & fees required. This is especially important in many manufacturing industries (waste) and restaurants/cafes/bars (food handling). Australian Recording Industry Association (ARIA) fees are also important to consider if you are playing live or recorded music. There are also specific registrations required for real estate agents and car dealers that vary from state to state.

Workers Compensation Insurance

If you have employees or contractors who provide only labour services, it is essential that you register for Workers Compensation Insurance. The rules for Workers Compensation Insurance have changed in the past few years and not only include employees and individual contractors but in many instances, may include contractors operating as a Company or a Trust and related entities. It is essential that you speak to your accountant to determine who is required to be registered or registered for Workers Compensation. Each state has different laws so these need to be determined separately, particularly if you are operating in several states.

ATO Registrations

As mentioned in Chapter 12 – Different Tax Types, there are various ATO registrations that you will need to undertake:

- Australian Business Number (ABN)

- Goods & Services Tax (GST)

- Pay as You go Tax (PAYG)

- Fringe Benefits Tax (FBT)

- Fuel Tax Credits (FTC)

The good news is that you can do all of them by going to:

https://www.ato.gov.au/business/registration/register-your-new-business/

This can be a bit of a challenge if you are unsure about the correct registration for your entity type so it is advisable to spend a little and get your Accountant to do the registrations for you so that it is all done correctly. You should also register for an AUSkey at the same time which will allow you to lodge your Business Activity (BAS) statements online. If you are going to use the ATO Clearinghouse for superannuation payments for employees, this can be set up here too.

There is special legislation relating to wine, fuel and luxury cars. The above mentioned link has another link to these details but as always, speak to your accountant.

Trademarks, Intellectual Property & Patents

Trademarks

These are usually the business/company name and logo/brand. Once a name is registered it is protected but you also need to register the business logo to ensure that it is not copied by your competitors. It is worthwhile getting advice from a trademark specialist and/or an accountant.

If you copy something that someone else has trademarked, then you could be up for massive fines that are likely to result in you having to close your business. While it is possible to do these registrations yourself, there are specialists that cover this type of registration and one of the best that I know of is Geoff Moller www.geoffmoller.com. Not only does Geoff give lots of free advice on his blog but he is a font of all knowledge on all things Trademark. IP Australia is the governing body of trademarks in Australia www.ipaustralia.gov.au and they have lots of interesting information on their website.

Intellectual Property

Intellectual Property (IP) is a collective name for trademarks, copyright and patents. Whilst there are specific laws governing each of these, it is important to consider confidentiality and "trade secrets". This is especially important if you have employees who have access to confidential information and might also be relevant in dealings with your customers and suppliers. Confidentiality should be a condition of employment and should always be considered when engaging with customers and suppliers, particularly in a manufacturing environment.

If you think that these circumstances might be relevant to your business, you need to consult with specialists that can assist you in drafting the necessary agreements.

Patents

If you have designed or created something that is unique to your business, you should consider patenting it to protect you from others copying your idea or design. This is however, not easy because it is often difficult to prove the uniqueness of your idea or design. There are different types of patents including local and international and I am afraid that there is no substitute for obtaining legal advice on this issue. It will be well worth it and could save you significant time and money in the long term.

To Do:

1. **Search the Business Name Register to determine if your name is available.**

2. **Determine what other registrations you need and contact Councils/Industry Bodies where necessary.**

3. **Get your Accountant or Tax Agent to complete your ATO registrations.**

4. **Review your Logo and procedures and consider trademarks and patents.**

5. **Consider the extent to which confidentiality is important to your business and take steps to protect yourself both now and in the future.**

CHAPTER 6

PROCESSES AND PROCEDURES

Most of the other chapters in this book mention processes and procedures and in some ways this chapter is perhaps one of the most important in the book. John Warrillow author of "Built to Sell: Creating a Business That Can Thrive Without You", summed it up perfectly when he said, *"I think business owners should build their business to sell from day one"*. This means in essence that everything that you do in your business such as production and selling and administration (processes), and everything that you expect your employees to do (procedures), needs to be documented. This is commonly referred to as an "Operations Manual". There are three reasons why this is important:

1. Should something happen to you or one of your staff you can easily employ someone to take over the role.

2. Documented procedures improve efficiencies and enable you to exercise better control over your business.

3. Should you at a later stage, wish to sell the business, it will be much easier for a purchaser to walk in and pick up from where when you left off.

The best way to develop a procedure is to create a flow chart outlining the steps to be taken in each procedure. I personally like to use a whiteboard and sticky notes (you can buy them in proper flowchart shapes but it's not essential) to flowchart what happens, thus allowing you to move and change them as you need to.

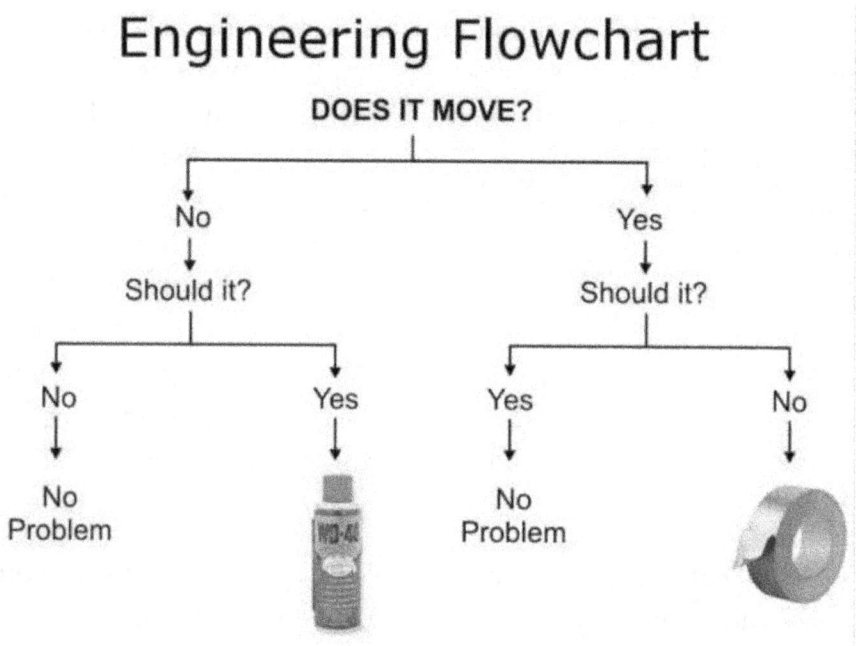

Once it's finalised, take a picture and transfer it to a document to create the procedure. Where possible include a diagram of the procedure in your document or even a copy of the photo of the whiteboard. If you already have staff, include them in the creation of these procedures as they may have a better knowledge of what they do and how they do it than you do. Don't be scared to include staff in a robust discussion about what is done and why it's done, often you may change a procedure resulting in a better outcome.

If you are planning on building a business that you are ultimately able to step out of, or scale-down your personal involvement, it is important that your processes and procedures are easily understood so that the necessary skills and knowledge can be transferred to new employees/owners. Any type of business, particularly a service business that relies totally on the skills and knowledge of the individual owner, would be very difficult to sell without documented processes and procedures.

Office Processes

Everything that happens in your office needs to have a procedure. While initially it may be you that does everything within the business, your goal should be to build your business to a level where you can delegate the day to day administration to someone else and concentrate on operational activities that you really enjoy doing in your business. Everything to do with your office needs to back up your customer service mantra.

The main areas that require documentation here are:

1. Telephone Procedures

Every single person that answers a phone in your business needs to answer it in the same manner. They need to know the process for dealing with incoming calls and the procedures for putting phone calls through. This includes how to deal with customers and suppliers and where phone calls need to be transferred to for every type of situation. Standard scripts are an ideal way to ensure that everyone is on the same page.

2. Mail Procedures

Imagine a situation where a letter arrives in the mail from a potential customer asking for information about your products and services or there is a warning letter from your bankers about a pending review of your facilities. If these matters are not dealt with efficiently, it could result in a loss of business or an embarrassing situation with your bankers. As discussed later under "banking procedures", opening incoming mail plays an important role in the financial controls of the business so it is important that proper procedures be put in place to deal with incoming and outgoing mail.

The detail that you go to in your mail procedure depends on your business and your capacity for paperwork. Ideally all incoming mail should be logged before being given to the appropriate person. This ensures that should there be follow-up required, there is an audit trail of who received what. There should also be a record of outgoing mail, so that should there be a query from someone not receiving mail, you have a record of when it was posted and to what address.

3. Bookkeeping Procedures

The idea of a bookkeeping system is to record all the transactions within your business to allow you to effectively manage your business and ultimately assist with preparation of taxation lodgements, whether they are income tax or GST. Bookkeeping procedures entails the processes of taking source documents such as invoices and inputting them into your bookkeeping system. It would document who is responsible for what action and who they report to which should reduce fraudulent activities by making different people responsible for different activities. This is discussed in detail in Chapter 14 – Internal Checks.

4. Banking

It is essential that banking procedures dovetail into your bookkeeping procedures. Ideally, the person that opens your mail should not be the person that is responsible for banking your takings. This will ensure that any cheques or money received goes through the hands of two people and lessens the risk of theft. It may sound absurd in a small business to segregate those roles, but there have been numerous instances of administration staff and bookkeepers in particular, who have taken advantage of non-existent procedures and internal checks to rip off substantial amounts from small businesses.

5. Debt Collection Procedures

Unless you are a "cash business" such as a restaurant or hairdresser, there will ultimately come a time in your business when you will need to grant credit to some or all of your customers. This involves a certain element of financial risk which is covered in more detail in the chapter on "Cash Flow Management". Suffice it to say, it's important for you to have standard procedures for following up outstanding invoices to ensure that they are paid on time This does not mean that we going to send round a bikie with a big hammer, it is simply a process to ensure that the customer is made aware of the outstanding debt and to try and arrange prompt payment of this debt to you.

Generally, the process starts with a gentle reminder through to actual debt collection or depending on the size of the debt, lodgement of the small claims in your state. Keep in mind that it is possible to automate this process using products such as "Chaser" or "Debtor Daddy". It is essential, regardless of whether your debt collection is manual or automated, that the same process is followed for all debtors and that there is consistency throughout your business. There is more on debt collection in Chapter 8 – Cash Flow Management.

6. Document Management

The procedures for the recording of information and filing of this information should be consistent for all employees or contractors of your business. This not only relates to invoices and receipts, but also phone messages, emails, and general discussions with clients. A system needs to be in place, not only to document all interactions with customers to ensure consistency but also the tracking of discussion and the ability for someone else to pick up where other staff members left off should they be away for a day or week or permanently. Products such as Receipt Bank www.receipt-bank.com and Shoeboxed www.shoeboxed.com assist with the bookkeeping side of recordkeeping, and there are also several packages available to assist you in keeping notes and files and also emails. Dropbox, Evernote, and other Customer Relationship Management (CRM) packages may also be of assistance.

Customer Service

Every contact that any of your staff have with your customers, needs to be the same. This means that all staff are in line with the mission of your business and your culture of how you treat customers. Ideally, all customers should be treated as if they are going to make a million-dollar purchase.

All areas can be templated regarding customer service, including telephone, customer feedback and complaints. Where possible try to ensure that all feedback is acted upon. It is also ideal to act promptly on all complaints and have a system that tries to delight a client, even those that complain.

Marketing and Sales

All marketing and sales procedures should also be documented. It ensures that everyone involved in marketing approaches customers in the correct way and in the same manner resulting in an awesome customer experience. These procedures not only include the interaction with customers but also the procedures for follow-up of the actual processing of orders. This ensures that once the salesperson receives an order, it is recorded on the system correctly to allow production to do its thing.

Chapter 2 – Marketing, delves deeper into the actual processes that need to be followed up, especially regarding automation of information gathering & customer retention. A good procedure to have here relates specifically to your website and automatic emails – how to create an email sequence and landing pages on your website. All should be done exactly the same way with the same branding features and could be created by anyone following a procedure. Naturally the content writing is something entirely different.

Production

It is essential that procedures are created for each and every process within your production line. It allows you to think ahead, possibly before you even start the business as to how are you are going to approach production. Keep in mind that production relates as much to service industries or intellectual property as it does for manufacturing or building. It is essential that all staff follow the same procedures in creating whatever it is that your business produces. Having awesome production procedures, will allow you to rapidly expand your business, should the opportunity arise. And always keep in mind the "built to sell" philosophy. Flowcharts are an awesome tool to show the flow of production.

Staff

A short list of the procedures that every business will need in relation to staff is listed below:

- Job description;

- Organisation chart;

- Advertising for staff;

- Interviewing potential staff;

- Hiring staff – including letters of offer and employment contracts;

- Codes of Conduct;

- Inducting staff;

- Staff training;

- Staff reviews;

- Staff incentive scheme(s); and

- Grievance procedures.

A good HR advisor can assist you with these procedures. If you want to try the DIY process for HR, a substitute for professional advice could possibly be Enable HR www.enablehr.com.au. This system allows you to use their templates and still update them to meet your circumstances, while having access to a fully trained HR consultant to review or give advice where possible.

Always consider contractors when dealing with staff issues and adapt the processes accordingly when possible. There is full description of staff and contractor issues in Chapter 10 – Staff.

To Do:

1. List all the processes in your business that need to be templated.

2. Source templates from other suppliers where possible (don't recreate the wheel).

3. Investigate software to make this process easier and more reliable.

CHAPTER 7

BOOKKEEPING AND RECORD KEEPING

Bookkeeping and record-keeping is certainly not everyone's cup of tea but the reality is that if you run a business of any kind, from start-up or a massive corporation, bookkeeping and record-keeping underpins everything that you do.

The important thing to keep in mind here is that everything that you order, buy and sell needs to be recorded. Paperwork at times can be a little overwhelming so in this chapter we will go through a few ideas of what you need to do and how to make it easier.

Bookkeeping is the art of keeping records of the transactions in your business. Traditionally these were done in big green ledgers, for those of us lucky enough to have been born more recently, bookkeeping has become a computerised process. There are a multitude of bookkeeping and accounting software programs available ranging from simple bookkeeping to sophisticated accounting and reporting packages. The most important thing is to find a system that suits you and the way that you operate.

Bookkeeping Packages

There are many bookkeeping packages on the market today and my favourite is Xero www.xero.com/au. Regardless of which package you choose, you need to ensure that it is easy to use and will operate well with the type of business you operate. For instance, a manufacturing business will have more sophisticated accounting needs than someone who runs a graphic design business. Xero is easy to use and can deal with both of these scenarios, Chapter 15 – Xero and its Ecosystem, explains more about how it all works. Don't just pick up something off the shelf, take the time to look at options and work with your accountant to find the best package for you.

Expense Receipts

It is important to keep in mind that every time you spend money for your business, you need to keep a receipt for that transaction. There are differences between the rules for income tax and GST purposes. The easiest way to keep on the right side of the ATO is simply to keep all receipts. If the thought of hundreds and hundreds of small receipts clogging up your filing and fading over time really doesn't resonate with you, there are two simple ways around it:

1. Scan each document and save them on your computer system.

2. Use an outsourced product which will not only store these documents for you, but also import them into an accounting package.

At present there are two leaders in Australia in this field. These are Shoeboxed www.shoeboxed.com and Receipt Bank http://www.receipt-bank.com. Both of these products are quite similar, the main deciding factor being whether you actually want the paper copies of your receipts returned to you or not. More information on these valuable resources is discussed in Chapter 15 – Xero and its Ecosystem.

Sales Receipts

It is equally important to keep valid records of your sales. If you are a shop or a business that uses registers, the ATO requires that you keep your till reads for 5 years after the year end of your tax return. This is an absolutely huge amount of paper to be storing for that length of time. A simple way to resolve this problem is to use a computerised system such as "Vend" www.vendhq.com which will automatically store till receipts and also import the daily sales directly into your Xero system. Another option is to scan all the documents and store them electronically, keeping in mind that they still need to be accessible in 5 years so make sure your backups are regular.

Even if you wish to keep the paper till receipt, you need to find a system that is going to work for you to input your daily sales into your accounting package.

Bank Accounts

All business transactions from bank accounts, credit cards, loans, PayPal and any other business related accounts need to be processed. Depending on your business structure, you may have bank accounts in your own and/or business name. It is essential, that you keep your business transactions separate from your personal account by operating a business bank account. This account does not need to be listed as a business account at the bank, and in some instances there may be less bank fees by opening a personal account. Failure to separate your personal affairs from the business will result in confusion and inaccurate figures not to mention the cost of sorting out the mess at a later stage.

Ideally, it is much easier to choose a bank that has system that is compatible with your accounting system. Xero links to most banks and building societies but some work better than others so if you have a choice, choose one that links well.

Payroll Records

Payroll records are different to normal taxation records, in that they need to be kept for a minimum of 10 years. This includes timesheets, employment contracts, and any other records regarding employees' performance. More information on payroll record-keeping and payroll in general is included in Chapter 10 – Staff.

A final note on payroll, is that it's well and truly worth the money to have an experienced payroll Bookkeeper set up your system for you. This ensures total compliance with all awards and also ensures that the processing system is easy for you to use moving forward.

While bookkeeping may seem scary to some, it is quite easy to make it a simple and painless process. You need to set up procedures in your business that assist you to collate the information required to record what is actually going on in your business. These include sales, expenses, outstanding accounts payable (creditors) and receivable (debtors), as well as payroll. It is something that many business owners don't enjoy but you need to be able to keep your finger on the pulse.

You also need to work out whether your time could be spent more effectively working "on" your business in critical areas like sales and operations as opposed to working "in" the business on administration and bookkeeping. Services such as The Bookkeeper Hub allow for total outsourcing of your bookkeeping systems. It may be worthwhile investigating these options to see if you can take this process out of your business and give you more time to do the things that matter.

To Do:

1. Choose an accounting package to use (Xero is my choice).

2. Identify ways of using technology to assist in collating invoices and expenses.

3. Assess whether you should outsource your bookkeeping.

CHAPTER 8

CASH FLOW MANAGEMENT

Cash is as vital to business as oxygen is to life. A business without sufficient cash behind it is doomed to fail. When thinking about cash and cash flow in your business, there are two types of cash that you need to think about. Firstly, there is start-up capital and secondly ongoing cash flow. In Chapter 1 we discussed business viability and provided a link to a basic cash flow budget. In this chapter we go into more detail on the different items to consider when trying to project your cash flow.

Start-Up Capital

Start-up capital is the cash that you require to set up your business initially. Ideally, the initial investment should be made from you first before looking to others to invest. Outside investors including banks, will always look to the business owner having "skin in the game". You should also bear in mind that having an outside investor will probably result in you foregoing some control of your business, but it also may bring other opportunities.

No matter where the cash comes from to start your business, it is essential that you create a budget for what needs to be spent, when it is going to be spent, and how it is going to be spent. It's important here to think about what you really need. That sounds a bit silly but let me put it to you like this, do you need the $3000 mahogany office table when you could quite as easily go to the local second-hand store and buy a perfectly good office desk for $100? Although you have grand plans for your business, you need to think small and thrifty. Also consider Software as a Service (SAAS) or "cloud" programs rather than purchasing desktop based programs where possible, they allow you to pay monthly for the services you need, not an up-front cash investment.

Ongoing (Working) Capital

Ongoing or "working" capital however, is a totally different beast. This is the day-to-day cash that you need to run your business, to pay your staff and pay your bills on time, to allow some extra cash for growth, and hopefully pay you at the end of the day. Being an accountant and bookkeeper, the obvious advice here is going to be – create a budget! That may sound like a cop-out but you need to ensure that you do the planning and think about exactly what it's going to cost you to run your business. You need to have a policy on what you can spend. This means that you don't go out and find something that looks cool and groovy and buy it because it <u>may</u> help you in your business. It means that you sit down and have a long hard think about it and then make a value decision on the impact it is going to have on your business, i.e. will you make more money by having it!

A good budget, will not only give you an indicator of your predicted income and expenditure (cash flow) but also the timing of these cash flows. It will factor in your trading terms for sales and payments as well as statutory payments such as BAS Statements and Superannuation.

Keeping Your Finger On the Pulse

Keeping your finger on the pulse of your business's cash flow is one of the most important things that you need to do as a business owner. Simply running by the seat of your pants and judging by the amount of cash that is in your bank account, is not how to run a business. As we discussed when we looked at processes and procedures, there needs to be a set of written procedures for invoicing, and the receipts and payments of cash so that the information is readily available. In order to have up-to-date information on where your business is heading, you need to have an accounting system that is updated regularly so that you can keep an eye on your cash flow. This was covered previously in the bookkeeping section and in more detail in Chapter 15 – Xero and its Ecosystem. I cannot say enough times that a cloud-based accounting system such as Xero will allow you to keep your finger on the pulse.

Debtors Management

Unless you are a cash business such as a restaurant or retail shop, you will inevitably come under pressure from your customers to supply them on "credit". This creates potentially significant risks for the business because you might have to pay your suppliers before you get paid by your customers. This could be the result of the terms that you allow your customers being different from those allowed by your suppliers. Alternatively, your customer might pay you later than agreed but you still have to pay your suppliers on time. Managing this is a good example of "cash flow management".

Let's look at the vital elements of Debtors Management:

1. Trading Terms

This is the time listed on your invoices or formal engagement that states the time given for your customers to pay. Retail shops generally have payment upfront. This means the customer comes in, buys the product and pays on the spot. Some industries such as building and construction insist on an upfront payment to start a project and then schedule regular payments with a final payment on completion. My suggestion to you is that if you are in a service industry, you consider either upfront payments or some type of scheduled payments to allow you to plan your cash flow.

Important considerations in granting credit are:

1.1 Size and reputation of the customer.

1.2 Reliable references of other suppliers.

1.3 Security given by the customer.

Well established credit terms give you the certainty of knowing when you are going to be paid.

2. Ease of Payment

Ideally you should make it as easy as possible for your clients or customers to pay you. It might sound like a trivial thing but having your bank account details on the invoice means that a person is in a position to pay you as an invoice is received. EFTPOS facilities, or payment gateways such as PayPal, Eway or Stripe which allow for the customer to simply click through to a gateway and pay the invoice directly from a credit card are other payment methods that should ideally be made available to customers.

Many of these services dovetail nicely into the Xero package, allowing you a distinct advantage in the collection of your debts because your customers can click straight from their invoice to the payment gateway, enticing them to pay earlier. There are other options available regarding payment. For example, a direct debit through products such as Ezidebit which to allows the regular payments to be deducted from the client's bank account or credit card.

Another option is invoice funding. A number of banks and individual companies provide these facilities where you are paid upfront for the invoice as it is raised, and then the customer is direct debited over a set number of payments. In this situation the customer pays the interest.

3. Monitoring Debtors

It is vitally important to get regular reports on what payments are outstanding. Most accounting systems provide what is called a "Debtors Age Analysis" which shows what is outstanding by each customer both in total and by period e.g. 30, 60, 90 days and over. A quick review of this analysis will soon tell you what is overdue and enables you to take immediate and effective action to follow up and secure payment.

4. Late Payment Procedures

For some the bane of their existence. It is vital that all businesses not only have a written credit agreement with each customer but also an effective procedure for following up late payment of invoices. In order to ensure that there are no disagreements regarding invoices, it is essential that you have written proof of the order and delivery. You should also find out from your customer where and how invoices are to be delivered.

Example 1: A company where a manager on site is able to order goods, but the invoice has to have a purchase order number and then be sent to head office. If you send the invoice to the site office, it could be weeks before it gets to head office and even enters the payment process. Sometimes it won't even make it to the head office!

Nobody likes chasing up late or bad debts. There are online applications available to assist you with process such as "Chaser" or "Debtor Daddy". It is important when evaluating these applications to think about the impact that this will have on your customers. Generally, they allow you to tailor not only payment terms but the tone or wording of your letters and reminders as well as the frequency of the reminders. There should also be provision for a manual override process that allows flexibility in the sending of reminders. It may sound stupid to have a manual process for an automated system, but if you have a client who has not paid for a valid reason and you have decided to give them some extra terms, you don't want to damage that relationship by your system sending out an automated nasty collection letter. Furthermore, the last thing that you need is for a major customer to get a stern reminder when they have already paid!

5. Interest on Late Payments

Consider whether you should seek interest on late payments, bearing in mind the potential difficulties in recovering it. In order to do this, there needs to be a clause in your engagement or credit terms that states that this will happen. Then you need to set up a process for interest to be calculated and charged. Ideally this should dovetail with your payment reminder process which, together with a "practiced eye" overview, should take the pressure off your admin team.

6. Actual Debt Collection

At some time unfortunately we all need to resort to debt collection to ensure payment of unpaid invoices. Different states have different processes, which vary depending on your industry and also on the value of the debt that is owed. Some processes you can do yourself, others need the assistance of the debt collection agency. The best suggestion that I have for you here, is to speak to your Mentor and also other business colleagues to get referrals to debt collection agencies in your area.

Debtors management can be complex and if not done effectively, can cripple a business. Whilst I have outlined the critical areas involved in managing your debtors, you should seek help to ensure that you set up effective systems to control this vital element of your cash flow.

Stock Management

If your business carries significant stock, then it is essential that these items are measured and controlled on a regular basis. Carrying too much stock ties up cash that may be needed to fund other costs of the business.

A standard measure is stock turnaround days. When combined with the days outstanding on your invoices, this is called "Lock-Up Days" and is the number of days in a cycle when stock is ordered or work commenced on a job until you are finally paid. There are various industry norms for lock-up days, so I suggest that you speak to your accountant regarding this to find out what they are in order for you to set targets and to manage your cash flow accordingly.

Whilst a good debt collection process will assist you in lowering your debtor days, you should always be looking at ways to reduce your stock. Ideas to help with this are "just-in-time". Just-in-time ordering means that you only order the stock needed when it is required. This will not always work for a retail business as it always needs to have goods on the shelves for display, however stock can still be minimised by having perhaps one or two items and the option to order more if required. Depending on the industry of your retail shop, customers may be happy to wait one or two days for their stock to arrive.

Generally, buying stock in bulk is cheaper than buying a just-in-time method. When deciding on your process regarding stock purchases, you need to do some simple maths.

Example 2: A Retail Store that sells printers – Say they can purchase printers for $200 each, however if they order ten at a time, the supplier will give them a discount of 2.5%, meaning they have to pay $1950 for the 10 printers. Whilst that sounds good, if the printers stay on the shelves for 6 months, and the $1950 has been funded by an overdraft at 9% interest, they will pay $87.75 in interest to save $50 on the stock purchase, not to mention they tie up $1950 of their cash that they could have been using to purchase other stock.

Work-In-Progress

Work in progress days is generally a bugbear for most service industries. What this means is that they have paid out either materials or wages for the product or service they are creating, and receiving payment for such at a much later date. This means the business is out of pocket until they get paid. What I suggest here, is to either have regular payment terms or drawdowns like the building industry or to enable payments to be received at agreed milestones along the way. If that is not possible, then there may be an opportunity to invoice upfront, and allow for regular payments of this invoice.

At the end of the day, you need to work out what system is going to work for you. If you have set targets, you need to monitor them regularly and work with your team to work out the most efficient way to run your business. "Cash is King", and the quicker you turn your stock and/or work in progress in your business into a sale that is paid for, the more valuable your business will be in the long-term and the better you will sleep at night!

To Do:

1. Create a meaningful cash flow budget.

2. Create procedures to assist in early payment of invoices & follow-up of late payments.

3. Review your Lock-Up Days and work on ways to reduce them.

CHAPTER 9

PREMISES

No matter what type of business you run, you still need to operate from somewhere. It is important to think about not only where you will operate from, but how your business is going to grow and what your needs will be in the future.

Home-Based

Many new businesses start out as home-based businesses. There is no problem with working from home but, there are a few considerations that you need to think about. The first is Council rules. Different councils have different rules on the number of employees or staff members that are allowed to operate out of a household dwelling. There might also be issues with noise from your machinery. It is important to check with your own Council if you are going to have staff on site, to ensure that you meet their requirements. Whilst these rules may seem inconvenient for you when you have say, a big garage, they have been put in place to ensure that your neighbours are not inconvenienced by the comings and goings of your staff and/or the operation of machinery.

If you work from home, there may be capital gains implications when you sell your house down the track. Currently the rules state that if you are running a business from home, regardless of whether you claim deductions or not, a CGT event will arise on the sale of the house. This needs to be discussed with your accountant, as the tax implications will depend on your individual status and tax law at the time.

This leads us to the deductions that are available for a home based business. Logically, if you are going to have to pay capital gains tax on your home when you sell it, you will want to ensure you are claiming all the deductions available to your business.

Home Deductions

Expenses for your home that you claim for your business generally relate the % of floor area of your house that is used in the business. This percentage can generally be easily calculated however; you need to remember that you must set aside a room for solely for business use. This means if you have a bedroom set up as an office that's okay, but if your office is merely in the corner of your lounge room it will be extremely difficult to claim the costs of running your house as business expenditure. Expenses that can be apportioned are:

Telephone – This is apportioned on a usage % and some kind of log needs to be kept.

Internet – This is the same as telephone.

Rates – Based on % floor area.

Electricity – Unless you have a separate meter for a shed or office in addition to your house, this is usually calculated based on an ATO rate on the no of hours the office is used during the week. If more than just an office is used, then some other kind apportionment needs to be discussed with your accountant.

Cleaning – Based on floor area.

Water Rates – Based on floor area.

Generally business insurance for business assets is separate to household policies, however if you are a Sole Trader, their might be an opportunity to claim a portion of your household insurance especially on business type assets if they are listed separately. It is advisable that you speak to your accountant in this regard.

Leased Premises

If you choose to operate out of leased premises, it is essential that you understand the ramifications of the lease that you are signing. Regardless of your entity structure, it is normal for the individuals concerned (sole trader, partners or directors) to guarantee that the rental payments will be paid until the lease is expires. There may be provisions within your lease that allow you to sublease areas to another business, however it is suggested that you seek legal advice on the correct interpretation of the terms of the lease. Some states require both an accountant and a solicitor to sign off on lease agreements prior to the lease executed.

Generally, with commercial premises, the lessee is required to pay not only a rental price or a rental fee but also all the outgoings of the building. This means that they need to pay the council rates and building insurance and in some instances depending on the type of property you are renting, their body corporate fees. It is essential that these costings are factored into your budgets and not just the base rental. If landlords find a shortage in the outgoings that they have charged you during a period, they are generally entitled to charge you for additional outgoings in later periods. It is also important that you read every lease thoroughly to ensure that the type of business that you are conducting is within the guidelines.

When starting your business, you need to think not only about what type of space you need now, but also how you intend to grow. There are many business incubators that are available around Australia and it may be viable for you to cohabit with other start-up businesses in the short term. In fact, it could be an extremely useful for networking, mentoring and general advice if the other tenants are in similar industries. If your business is one that relies on a lot of walk in traffic, then you need to ensure that your premises are situated in an area that people are walking past.

Virtual Premises

Another option available to you may be virtual premises. In thinking about this unique option, you need to consider what you can sell online, whether it be a service business or something that is downloadable, or is there actually stock you need to store. If you have goods that need storage, and distribution, then you need to consider a cost-effective way of storing these whilst at the same time allowing easy access to you and/or customers.

One last piece of information to remember is that regardless of your premises, ensure that you have the right insurances in place. This is discussed further on in Chapter 11 – Insurances.

To Do:

1. **Work out what kind of premises you need in the short to medium term.**

2. **If leased, make sure you read the lease documents carefully.**

3. **Get appropriate Legal and Accounting Advice.**

CHAPTER 10

STAFF

It would be really easy to write a whole book on staff, and in fact human resources or HR is a full degree course offered by many universities. It is well outside the realm of this book to be an absolute resource on the hiring and management of staff. It is important to note however, that at some stage your business will grow and you will need staff.

A well planned business can grow quickly into an organisation that requires you to employ staff. It makes sense for you to apply your skills in areas where the business will derive the greatest benefit. For example, completing the quarterly BAS returns might appear to save you money but could your time be spent more profitably on developing new customers, markets and/or products?

It is important to plan for staff when setting up the original business plan, and to think about what you will need them to do, when they can assist you, and how you can utilise them to make better use of your time. The easiest way to do this is to create an organisation chart, even if your name is listed under each job in the short term!

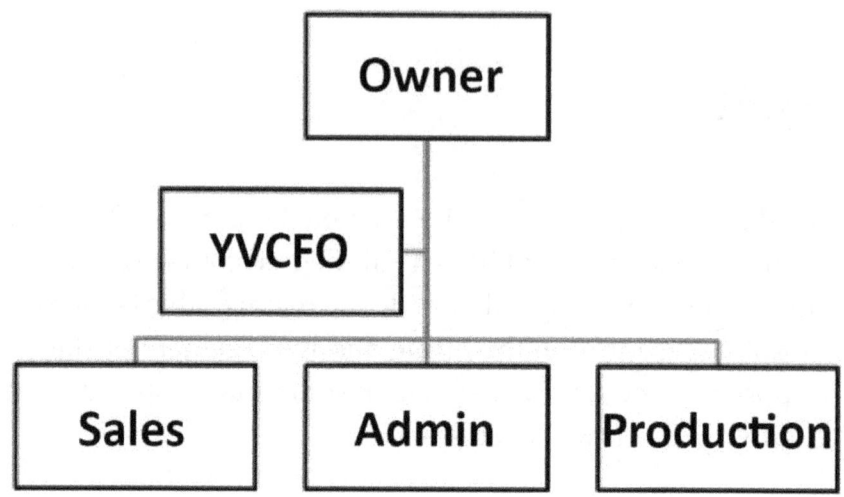

This will provide a basic plan for what staff you will need, their respective roles and who reports to whom. This will enable you to work out what each team member will actually do and to write detailed job descriptions that should dovetail with the processes and procedures outlined in the Operations Manual (Chapter 6 – Processes and Procedures). Generally, it is not possible for you to oversee all staff over all the hours of the day therefore it is essential that everything is documented so that job functions and responsibilities are clear to everyone. The actual creation of an Organisational Chart is quite easy; Excel has templates available within the program.

Employee vs Contractor

Over recent years, contractors seem to be making the headlines. All of us know of people who have worked for an organisation, have been made redundant and then all of a sudden are back in that organisation working as an external contractor. The reality is that under current tax laws there is no such thing as a contractor who only provides services to one company. There are special rules for contractors and both the ATO and Fair Work Australia have some good information & checklists to determine whether staff are actually contractors or employees:

https://www.ato.gov.au/Business/Employers/Preparing-to-engage-workers/Employee-or-contractor/

And

http://www.fairwork.gov.au/about-us/policies-and-guides/fact-sheets/rights-and-obligations/contractors-and-employees-whats-the-difference

The difference between an employee and a contractor is important because it determines whether Workers Compensation Insurance and/or Superannuation Guarantee is payable for that person. Workers Compensation is a state-based process and even States have different rules especially regarding contractors, so it is essential to check the rules that apply in your particular State. Another important distinction is that unlike employees, contractors do not fall under an Industry Award so rates can be more flexible and negotiable. Information on minimum pay rates, leave entitlements and individual awards can be found at www.fairwork.gov.au.

Outsourcing

Outsourcing is a massive opportunity. There are companies based overseas, predominantly in India and the Philippines that may offer an opportunity for you to outsource various procedures of your business. There are also websites such as www.upwork.com and www.fiverr.com which act as an online marketplace for employers and potential contractors. These outsourcing opportunities can be a useful and sometimes a cheap source of labour and can be used for either regular or one-off projects. An example of a regular project would be a Virtual Assistant, whilst a one-off may be creation of a logo or marketing brochure. It is important to read the rules and regulations regarding each of these sites, and ensure that you comply with their guidelines. Most of them provide client reviews and on request, you are able to view samples of each potential contractor's previous work which is essential in choosing the right contractor. In addition, I highly recommend face-to-face meetings via Skype or GoToMeeting prior to engaging with any outsourcing contractor. Whilst I cannot give any guarantees, I have used both Upwork and Fiverr on individual graphics projects where I don't have those skills and found the process generally easy to use and (almost) enjoyable.

Engaging your Employees and Contractors

When engaging a contractor or an employee, it is important that you match an employee to the role, not the role to the employee. This may be harsh, but nobody is indispensable.

Simply because you have a friend or family member who may be available to assist you, does not mean that they are necessarily the right person for the job. Once you define the role within your business, you'll be able to advertise for the right person. When interviewing for an important role in your organisation, it is important to think about your long-term plan and ensure that the employee is going to be the right "fit" for your organisation.

Example – Get the right people on the bus: Imagine you are driving a bus (your business) and you have a map of where you want to go (your business plan). When you pull up to the bus stop to take on passengers (staff), you need to ensure that you have the right person on the bus, i.e. he/she is going where you are going (the right mind-set). If they are not, don't let them on (don't employ) or if you discover after they have boarded (been employed) that they are going somewhere different, stop the bus and let the person off (let them go).

If you do need to let someone go it is essential that you do it in the correct manner and in a way that is legal. A good HR consultant can assist you with this.

Letter of Employment

Many business owners fall into the trap of employing someone without having the employee sign a letter of employment. I cannot stress too strongly the importance of doing this. I know that it is sometimes difficult to ask a friend or family member to sign an employment letter but this needs to be done to protect both parties in the event of a disagreement.

In addition to the standard clauses relating to role and responsibilities, rate of pay, superannuation, annual and sick leave, etc., the letter should also cover:

1. Confidentiality: The employee or contractor will be privy to a wide range of information that could be of value to your competitors not to mention any sensitive personal information. It is therefore vital that you ensure that the employee maintains an acceptable level of confidentiality both during and after their employment.

2. Restraint of Trade: Depending upon the type of business you are in, you should consider some form of restraint of trade for employees who leave your employ and might seek to start a similar business in your area and target your customers. There are restrictions on what business owners can do in terms of restraints of trade but you can get a degree of protection and I would strongly advise you to seek legal advice if this is important to your business.

3. Intellectual Property (IP): In many businesses, employees are involved together with the business owner, in developing "intellectual property". Unless this is protected, when an employee leaves your employ, they can use the IP for their own purposes and cause significant financial loss to your business. The Letter of Engagement should state that any IP developed during the period of employment with the business, remains the property of the business. Again, if this is important, seek legal advice.

The bottom line here is to have a letter of engagement that protects the interests of the business and the employee.

Minimum Wages

Australia has minimum wage standards. All businesses, regardless of their business structure, need to abide by these standards which not only provide fair pay and leave but also working conditions. As a general rule employees are entitled to 20 annual leave days a year and 10 personal leave days per year. Fair Work Australia www.fairwork.gov.au has a lot of information regarding employees and their entitlements and also a list of the most current awards and agreements. Search under the "awards and agreements" section to find the award that is the closest to your business. If in doubt, seek the advice of an HR consultant. It is also important to recognise that different industries or different work-sites may have individual enterprise bargaining or labour hire agreements. Enable HR www.enablehr.com.au can be a good source of information and can assist with ongoing HR obligations.

Payroll

Payroll is the process of determining and recording the wages, superannuation and PAYG Withholding for each employee on a weekly, fortnightly or monthly basis.

Generally, the wages payable is the more difficult of these to determine as it all depends on which award your employee is employed under and if there are different rates of pay for different types of work, i.e. there will usually be a different rate for working on a weekday compared to a weekend or a public holiday; or a meal-allowance to be paid if the employee works more than 8 hours. The awards are extremely specific so it is essential that your payroll system is created with the right functions to enable you to work these out correctly. Most accounting packages have payroll functions but these generally don't have the awards setup from the outset and these need to be created and linked to each individual employee. An experienced payroll officer or bookkeeper will be able to assist you with this. There are also specific payroll packages which for additional fees, can be utilised for this function but as mentioned above, the base information is available from Fair Work Australia.

Regardless of how you create your payroll processing, you need to be able to produce reports to determine the gross wages, allowances, PAYG Withholding and Superannuation Liability to meet legislative reporting requirements. A computerised payroll system can create PAYG Summaries at year end too because writing these by hand is a major time consuming exercise.

PAYG Withholding

Pay-As-You-Go Tax or PAYG needs to be deducted from employees' wages. This is discussed in further detail in Chapter 12 – Different Tax Types. These tables are available on the ATO website to determine how much tax to deduct. This site also has a PAYG calculator which can be used if you do not use an accounting package to calculate your payroll (which I don't recommend).

It is important to note here that when employing staff, there are two important things to be considered:

1. The entity employing the staff must be registered for PAYG, and

2. The employee needs to fill out a tax file number declaration form. The TFN declarations need to be ordered directly from the ATO. Presently the ATO does not have a pdf download available on its website, hopefully it will in the future.

The frequency of your PAYG Withholding payment to the ATO depends on the size of your payroll. If your PAYG Withholding is under $25,000 per year it is generally paid quarterly on your Business Activity Statement and due 28 days after the end of the quarter. If it is over $25,000 then it is due monthly (on the 21st of the following month) on either an Instalment Activity Statement or Business Activity Statement, depending on your GST Registrations.

Superannuation Guarantee Charge

This is something else to consider when employing staff. Any employee (not a true contractor) over the age of 18 who earns more than $450 per month needs to have superannuation paid on their behalf. Any employee under 18, who works 30 hours per week, also needs to have superannuation guarantee paid on their behalf. The Superannuation Guarantee Levy (SGC) is currently 9.5% of their ordinary times earnings. At the time of writing, this SGC rate will remain unchanged until 1/7/2018 when it will increase by 0.5% each year until it reaches 12% from 1/7/2022. The ATO have a good checklist of what constitutes ordinary times earnings:

https://www.ato.gov.au/Business/Employers-super/How-much-to-pay-and-when-to-pay/Ordinary-time-earnings/Checklist-for-salary-or-wages-and-ordinary-time-earnings/

Superannuation is dealt with more fully in Chapter 12 – Different Tax Types.

Workers Compensation Insurance

It is mandatory that you set up a Workers Compensation Insurance policy prior to employing staff. Workers Compensation Insurance provides safety for employees who are who are injured at or travelling to or from work and is run on a State by State basis. Once you have established your policy, remember to advise your state-based board if your payroll increases above what you advised them when you initially set it up. Generally, there is an initial premium which is then adjusted on the basis of your final wages figure at the end of the year. Some states offer funding to pay off workers' compensation premiums but if they don't, there are external providers who can. Contact the Workers Compensation Board in your state to get a list of these providers. If your employee is injured, there is a process to follow and it is essential that you contact the Workers Compensation Board as soon as practicable after the incident occurs. This is covered again in Chapter 11 – Insurances.

Payroll Tax

Payroll Tax is a state based tax levy based on the total annual payroll. Payroll Tax is discussed in detail in Chapter 12 – Different Tax Types.

Payroll Programs

It is suggested that your choice of accounting package includes a payroll capability. Xero does this quite easily and quite simply. The more work that you can get the computer to do for you, the less chance there will be of errors occurring in this important area. There are a number of Xero Add-Ons available to assist you with rostering, time records and transferring those times into timesheets in the Xero package for payroll processing, Deputy www.deputy.com seems to be the leader in this area at the time of writing. For more information on this checkout www.bookkeeperhub.com.au who can process your payroll for you or www.xero.com/au regarding the add-ons available.

To Do:

1. Work out what you want your staff need to do.

2. Create a position description and procedures and policies for that person.

3. Determine whether you need an employee, contractor, or outsourced contractor.

4. Advertise for the role, interview and make sure you pick the right person to board your bus.

5. When employing a staff member, ensure that you do the following:

   a. Locate the relevant awards and pay them accordingly.

   b. Register for PAYG.

   c. Ensure that a Tax File Number Declaration is filled in and transmitted to the ATO, either through your accounting package or in paper (Xero lodges these electronically).

   d. Take out a Workers Compensation Insurance policy.

   e. Source a payroll expert Bookkeeper to set up your payroll system or outsource it.

   f. Ensure you continue to meet the minimum wage guidelines.

6. Ensure that all wages are paid on time, superannuation is paid on time, and the correct PAYG is reported in the monthly or quarterly in your business activity statement.

7. If for some reason you find you have employed the wrong person for the job, get HR advice to ensure termination of this person is done correctly and legally. it is important for the longevity of your business that not only do you terminate this person quickly but you do it properly.

CHAPTER 11

INSURANCES

We have all heard about the dodgy insurance salesman, but in all seriousness, is essential that you make sure you have the right insurance for your business. Below is a brief in overview of the different types of business insurances that you need to consider for your business.

Public Liability Insurance

Public liability insurance is a general insurance that protects the public should they injure themselves on your premises. If you have an office, a shop, showroom or workshop, it is essential that you take out public liability insurance. Insurance is provided by a wide range of suppliers and the easiest way to organise a policy is to speak to an insurance agent who will be able to find one to suit your needs. Some industries require minimum public liability insurance, as do some business premises. Banks also often wish to see your insurance policies when providing funding.

Professional Indemnity Insurance

Professional Indemnity Insurance (PI) provides surety to the clients of service industries on the standard of their work. Generally different industry registrations or bodies have minimum requirements and minimum levels of the PI insurance. An example of this insurance would be a bookkeeper who provides BAS agent services who needs to provide a minimum cover of $2 million.

General Insurance

General Business Insurance covers items such as plant and equipment and can also be extended to cover items such as glass and motor burnout. Any business which has any type of premises and/or plant and equipment, needs to ensure that they do take out this insurance. There are a variety of insurance providers who cover this type of insurance however, it is often easier to use the one insurance agent for all of your types of insurance. Their job is to check with the different providers and get you the best deal. There are also many online insurance providers, but it is essential when looking at these policies that you specify that the plant and equipment is used for business purposes.

Income Protection Insurance

Income Protection Insurance is generally taken out by an individual to cover their wages or their business income should something unexpected happened. As a rule of thumb business owners are not covered by Workers Compensation Insurance and should they have an injury or some kind of unforeseen medical issue, they need to ensure that their earnings are covered. This is different to business loss of income cover which is also recommended. Your insurance broker should be able to advise you on the best type of insurance for your needs.

Transit Insurance

Businesses that ship goods should consider transit insurance prior to shipping. Whether goods are shipped around the world or around the corner, this insurance covers stock in transit. Imagine if the truck that was carting your product to a supplier had an accident and caught fire, whilst you possibly may be able to obtain some relief from the transport company, chances are their documentation which you didn't really read, says all risk is on the owner of the goods!

Buy/Sell Insurance

Buy/Sell Insurance allows a shareholder in a Company to take out insurance on the lives of the other shareholders to ensure that in the event of the death of a shareholder, he/she will have the funds to buy out the deceased shareholder from his/her estate. The same principle applies to Partnerships and Unit Trusts. Generally, a good Partnership, Unit Trust or Shareholders Agreement will require that this insurance be taken out.

Example 1: Bill and Mary are partners in the business. Bill takes out life insurance on Mary, with the beneficiary of this insurance being Bill. If something were to happen to Mary, the insurance policy would pay a death benefit to Bill, which would allow him to buy Mary's share of the business from her estate.

This is an important insurance that is often overlooked as a cost saving measure when starting a business, however it is essential that not only are the agreements and insurances are in place but that the insurances are updated on a regularly based for changes in the value of the business.

At the end of the day, each individual business owner is responsible for taking out the insurances they believe they need. Unless it is a bank requirement, it may be something that slips to the back of your mind or does not seems important. I can assure you, having seen it in in real life, that keeping up with your insurance payments can either make or break a business should the unexpected happen.

Example 2: Bill's brother Barry is a truck driver who is doing it tough so decides not to renew his truck insurance. If his truck is involved in an accident and written off, not only does he have a smashed truck that he is unable to use to earn an income, but he still needs to make repayments to the finance company until that loan is paid out.

All I can suggest to you is to get in touch with a good insurance broker, as not only can they secure a good deal, but they can often organise finance for your insurance payments over nine or 12 months, easing your cash flow. It is important to keep in mind, that even though you have a good insurance broker, obtaining a second opinion on different insurances will keep their pencils sharp! Ask your friends or colleagues for a referral to help you find a good broker.

Tips:

1. **Work out what types of insurances you need in your business.**

2. **Speak to a good insurance agent/broker to get quotes for your planning.**

3. **Take out insurances that cover your needs and review these regularly for increases in value.**

4. **Ensure your insurances are always paid on time.**

CHAPTER 12

DIFFERENT TAX TYPES

It has been said in there are two things in life that are certain – death and taxes. While there are sections in this book that discuss the effects that death may have on your business, taxes are something that all of us need to deal with to make sure that we remain on the right side of the Australian Taxation Office (ATO). A good accountant can not only help you comply with tax office rules but can also assist with future planning to legally minimise your taxation liabilities.

There are numerous types of Taxes in Australia and these can be quite overwhelming for a new business owner.

Please not that all the advice given on Income Tax matters within this book are of a general nature and specific instruction should be requested from your personal tax advisor before any decisions are made.

INCOME TAX

Whilst Income Tax is something that you have possibly dealt with during your lifetime as an employee, it will have different implications for you as a business owner. This will depend on factors such as the type of entity that you use to run your business, and the ability to income split between different family members. Income Tax is discussed further in Chapter 13 – Income Tax Basics.

GOODS AND SERVICES TAX (GST)

What is GST?

Unless you were in business in the year 2000 or have been trained in the idiosyncrasies of GST since, chances are that as a new business owner you have no knowledge of how the GST system works. Basically GST is a tax on goods and services, the main idea being that the "end user" or consumer pays tax on goods and services that they use. Logically, this tax means that the more people earn, the more they spend, and therefore the more tax (GST) that they will pay. The premise of this book is not to be a GST manual but generally an idea of how it works for small business.

If you are in business, you are basically an unpaid and un-superannuated tax collector. What this means is that your business is required to report either monthly, quarterly, or annually on the amount of GST received and paid by the business. This reporting is done on a Business Activity Statement (BAS). If your business turnover is over $75,000, then it is legislated that you must register for GST, and you must prepare the BAS statements. If your turnover is less than $75,000 you can choose whether to register or not.

Claiming GST paid

If you are registered for GST, you are entitled to deduct any GST paid on goods and services used in the ordinary course of running your business. There are however, specific requirements that must be complied with when claiming GST paid.

For GST purposes, all expenses you incur over $82.50 need a valid "tax invoice" that needs to include:

- Your business name, address and ABN.

- Say "Tax Invoice".

- Invoice Number

- Purchaser's Name

- Date of Transaction.

- Brief description of what is sold.

- Sale price or amount paid.

- GST component – either "total price includes GST" or Price + GST = Total.

- Date due for payment/payment terms.

- Method of payment, including bank accounts for EFT if you want to be paid that way.

- If the invoice is over $1000 you need to have the address of the purchaser on the invoices as well.

Failure to comply with these requirements could result in the GST claim being disallowed.

Some Exemptions

There are some goods and services that are GST Free, a few are listed below. A full list of GST Free goods and services can be found at:

https://www.ato.gov.au/Business/GST/When-to-charge-GST-(and-when-not-to)/GST-free-sales

These may include:

- Some education courses, course materials and related excursions or field trips.

- Some medical, health and care services.

- Exports

- Sales of businesses as going concerns.

- Basic food

Basic food is something that always confuses people. If in doubt, check the following link:

www.ato.gov.au/Business/Consultation--Business/In-detail/Food-industry/Food-classification-for-GST/GST-food-guide/

If you are selling goods and services that are GST free and your turnover is less than $75,000 then it may be beneficial to voluntarily register as you will receive refunds of the GST, you have spent on running your business.

Reporting

In general, if your bookkeeping systems are set up correctly and you have received training or advice on how to use them, the preparation of a Business Activity Statement is reasonably straightforward. It is important however to remember the lodgement deadline for the statements to ensure that you do not receive late fees if these are lodged late. A schedule of the lodgement deadlines is listed below:

Period	Due Date
1 July to 30 September	28 October
1 October to 31 December	28 February
1 January to 31 March	28 April
1 April to 30 June	28 July

As you can see, the lodgement date deadline is the 28th of the month after the end of the quarter, however there is an extra month grace given for the December quarter as the ATO does realise that the nation as a whole takes significant holidays over this period.

The ATO is moving towards mandatory electronic lodgements of BAS. In order to do this, you need to register for an AUSkey which will allow you to log into the ATO Portal and lodge your BAS. In time you will possibly be able to lodge directly from your accounting system but this is presently under development.

Pay As You Go Tax (PAYG)

The next most common taxation that business owners need to be understanding is Pay As You Go (PAYG). There are two types of PAYG, there is PAYGW which is the tax withheld from employees pay, and PAYGI instalments which is a prepayment of income tax for an entity or individual.

PAYGW

PAYG Withholding is calculated on an employee's wages based on the individual tax scale of rates. This tax scale can be calculated weekly, fortnightly or monthly and is available on the ATO website at: https://www.ato.gov.au/Calculators-and-tools/Tax-withheld-calculator/

These can either be downloaded or there is a calculator that you can use to calculate PAYG withholding. However, if you use a computerised payroll system, these generally calculate PAYG withholding required for each period, provided that they are set up correctly. It is important to note that the ATO does regularly change individual tax rates and it is important to ensure that your program is up to date with the most current updated rates. Most desktop programs require an annual upgrade to ensure compliance with the annual tax rates with a corresponding fee, however most cloud-based programs provide this free of charge as it is included in your monthly subscription.

Like GST, PAYG deducted from employees' wages by businesses, must be paid to the ATO on a monthly or quarterly basis. There is a separate section on the back of the BAS Statement for recording gross wages and PAYG Withholding.

Another thing to remember is that annual PAYG summaries and need to be provided to your employees by 14 July each year. These summaries can either be computer-generated or handwritten. There are significant time savings to be made by using a computerised accounting package to create the summaries. Depending on the payroll program used, it may be possible to lodge copies directly from your computer with ATO.

PAYGI

A PAYG Instalment is a prepayment of the current year's tax. If you are an individual who has a tax bill over $4000 or a company with tax payable, the ATO will automatically register you in the PAYGI system. This means that on a quarterly basis, you will need to pay an instalment or prepayment to the ATO for the current year's Income Tax. This can be either a predetermined amount or a % of your turnover as advised by the ATO. It is possible to change the calculations of PAYGI if your circumstances change but if you vary it and the end result is out by more than 10%, the ATO can apply penalties. There is also an annual PAYG instalment for individuals in limited circumstances.

Superannuation Guarantee Charge (SGC)

Superannuation Guarantee Charge or SGC is something else that all employers must be aware of. The general rule is that any employee over the age of 18 years who earns more than $450 in a month must have superannuation paid on their behalf. Superannuation is required to be paid by the 28th day following the end of the quarter. Currently superannuation is 9.5% of the employee's ordinary time's earnings. There are two things to consider here:

1. The actual SGC rate does change from year to year. Recent governments have changed the timing of increases in the super guarantee charge. It is essential to check with the ATO that the rate has not changed from prior years. As with PAYG, this rate is generally updated by computerised accounting systems.

2. It is important to consider what constitutes ordinary times earnings. As a general rule this is the normal wage paid to employee not including overtime or allowances, although it is essential that you check the ATO website:

https://www.ato.gov.au/Business/Employers-super/In-detail/Calculating-and-paying/Using-ordinary-time-earnings-to-calculate-the-super-guarantee/?page=2

... to ensure that what you are paying your employees does or does not constitute earnings applicable to the super guarantee.

Businesses that fail to pay their SGC obligations by the 28th of the month following the Quarter, have to lodge a super guarantee form. When lodging this form, the ATO will charge both administration fee and interest on the missed superannuation. If the superannuation payment is made within 28 days of the superannuation guarantee charge due date, the ATO will allow an offset of this amount, however interest and administration fees are still charged. It is important to note that any late payments of super guarantee charges are not tax-deductible, regardless of your entity type. It is also important to note that if you operate through a Trust or a Company, late SGC payments in the ATO may incur a director's penalty notice which means that the individual directors or trustees are personally liable for unpaid superannuation. The bottom line is that an Employer needs to ensure that Employee payments are kept up-to-date.

Superstream

From 1 July 2014 the government has been rolling out Superstream. It is mandatory for all business regardless of size from 1 July 2016. Superstream is designed to streamline the payment of superannuation guarantee payments directly into super funds and to cut down on red tape, and late payments. Perhaps I am a little cynical for, although it will provide some time savings for many employers, I personally believe that it is mainly to do with the ATO being able to check on the payment of SGC by employers. When choosing an accounting system, which is discussed throughout the book, it is recommended that you choose a system that is compatible with Superstream as it will make your life easier. To try to keep the Superstream as painless as possible for small business, the ATO has created a Small Business Superannuation Clearing House for businesses with less than 19 employees. Information about his can be found at:

https://www.ato.gov.au/Business/Employers-super/In-detail/Small-Business-Superannuation-Clearing-House/Using-the-small-business-superannuation-clearing-house/

Another thing to consider with the superannuation guarantee is that it not only covers employees but it may cover contractors as well. It is essential that you get professional advice regarding this as contractors that provide labour services only, need to be covered by super guarantee. It is generally recommended that any contractors that are covered by such agreements really should be PAYG employees rather than contractors. Currently there are rules for exempting contractors operating as companies from this requirement, however the ATO is looking at this and it is likely that amendments will be introduced eliminate such practices.

The ATO has provided a decision tool for the construction industry:

https://www.ato.gov.au/Calculators-and-tools/Building-and-construction-industry---employee/contractor-decision-tool/

Although this tool is specifically for the Building & Construction Industry, the same principles apply to other industries.

Fringe Benefits Tax (FBT)

Employers also need to be aware of Fringe Benefits Tax. This is basically a tax on any benefits that employees may receive that are not a cash wage. The most common benefits that employees may receive from a business are private use of a motor vehicle, low-cost housing, living away from home allowances, and entertainment benefits. There are various ways to calculate the benefit that an employee may receive and that is something that is really in the realm of your Accountant. It is important however for you as a business owner to know that this tax exists and to discuss this with your Accountant to ensure that the right records are being kept to prove or disprove any deemed benefit. Also, just to keep things interesting, the fringe benefits tax year goes from 1 April to 31 March which is different to the general income tax year.

A couple of easy rules of thumb to remember are:

- Any vehicle that is being provided to an employee needs to have adequate records as to the running costs and the business use of the vehicle. Generally, travel from home to work in the vehicle is non-claimable however there are exemptions for utilities in special circumstances, so check this with your accountant.

- Any irregular food and drinks provided to employees on site such as Friday afternoon drinks is generally claimable, however any food and drinks provided off-site such as the annual Christmas party is non-claimable.

- Drinks consumed with clients/non-employees can either be calculated under a 50-50 split method or a percentage method regarding the number of attendees, however documentation needs to be provided in each individual instance to show the number of attendees, employees and show which method is used. Any food or drinks consumed with non-employees is non-deductible.

- Entertainment benefits are in a league of their own and these refer to activities such as corporate boxes and may also include corporate golf days or training retreats. Seek advice from your Accountant.

- Also note that the definition of employees also includes spouses and children of an employee.

Payroll Tax

Payroll tax is a state-based tax levy is based on annual payroll. The actual thresholds vary from State to State but as a rough guide, if your payroll is under $800,000, you won't need to worry about this tax. It may seem strange to be mentioning this in a book about start-up businesses, but if your business is labour intensive then it is quite easy to reach the State level very quickly. This tax is generally levied on the basis of where the employee is actually working at the time. Something to be mindful of is that they will look at the aggregate of your payroll, and then the actual amount paid in each state to determine the liability. For more information on payroll tax specific to your State, "Google" Payroll Tax and your State to go directly to the relevant department as the names do change from state to state. Keep in mind also that anti-avoidance and grouping rules apply so you cannot simply have 5 companies with $200k payroll to get around it.

Generally, payroll tax is paid on a monthly basis, due around the 7th of the month.

Capital Gains Tax (CGT)

Capital Gains Tax is levied on any capital investment that is sold at a profit. Typical examples of this are the profit on the sale of shares or the sale of a business. As a rule of thumb, the difference between the cost of an investment and sale price less any sale or purchase costs, will give you a profit or loss on sale. If there is a profit on sale it will be taxable whereas if there is a loss on sale, there will be a capital loss which may be carried forward indefinitely until such times as you make a capital gain. Also, providing you don't operate as a company, there is a general 50% exemption of the capital gain if you owned the asset for more than 12 months. Keep in mind here that the date of sale is the date when the contract is signed, not the settlement date.

Capital gains on investments owned by a company are taxed in the company at a 30% level, although there are some small business exemptions which are discussed below. Any gains by sole traders, partnerships or trusts, are taxed at the individual tax rates of the individual, partner or beneficiary.

Small Business Exemptions

There are currently some exemptions for small businesses. Naturally you need to seek professional advice regarding capital gains but the rules regarding these as follows:

- 12 Month Exemption – As long as you have owned the asset for more than 12 months, the gain will be reduced by 50% (not companies).

- 50% Active Asset Exemption – If the asset is classed as an active asset, which means that it is used in producing income for the business, then an additional 50% exemption may be claimed.

- Retirement Exemption – It is possible in many circumstances to roll over the balance of any capital gain into retirement. If the individual involved is under 55 years of age, then the cash balance of this exemption must be paid into a superannuation fund. There is no tax paid by the super fund on receipt of this income, and the individual will pay no tax on the withdrawal of this fund. If the individual involved is over 55 years of age, then the cash may be paid to the individual free of tax.

- 15-Year Rule – Depending on your entity structure, if the asset in question has been actively used in creating income for a business for over 15 years, then the gain may be eligible for 100% exemption.

Example: Bill sold his takeaway shop for $100,000. As he and Mary had owned it for 8 years, they met the requirements for the 50% 12 Month Exemption as it was an active business then they were eligible for another 50% Exemption. As Bill and Mary were under 55, they could either then roll the remaining gain into a superannuation fund or pay tax on the balance, assuming they rolled into superannuation:

Sale Price	100,000
12 Month Exemption	(50,000)
Remaining Gain	50,000
50% Active Asset Exemption	(25,000)
Remaining Gain	25,000
Retirement Exemption	(25,000)
Taxable Capital Gain	0

Please note that the small business CGT exemptions have many varied owner requirements so it is absolutely essential that you speak to your accountant to determine what you are eligible for and if possible, to plan to obtain the most benefit legally possible.

To Do:

1. Work out if you need to be registered for GST.

2. If you employ staff, register for PAYGW.

3. Ensure you note the lodgement deadlines and have your paperwork completed prior to this date and the payments made by then.

4. Get specialised advice regarding your situation from your Accountant.

CHAPTER 13

INCOME TAX BASICS

Income Tax is the tax that is referred to when quoting death & taxes. Basically it is a tax on the taxable income of individuals and companies. Individuals have marginal tax levels depending on the level of their total "taxable" income, that are applied in working out the amount of tax that is payable. Companies however, currently run at a standard 30% (28.5% for small businesses) income tax on net profits. Partnerships and Trusts distribute their profits to the partners or beneficiaries who include this income in their own taxable incomes.

As a business owner is important that you know when your income tax is due for lodgement, keeping in mind that there are concessional lodgement dates if your returns are lodged by tax agents. Late lodgement penalties can be applied, and generally, if you lodge your tax return late in one year, it is required earlier in the following year. New entities may have a different lodgement date to existing entities so it is important to check your lodgement date with your tax agent/accountant (although a good tax agent will contact you first).

As mentioned before when dealing with PAYG, instalments of income tax are payable by all companies and by individuals who had over $4000 tax to pay in the previous year. These instalments are due on the same date as the quarterly BAS. If you are not registered for GST, then you will receive an Instalment Activity Statement (IAS) to lodge your payment.

As discussed in Chapter 12 – Different Tax Types, there are lots of taxes that a business owner needs to be aware of. The focus of this chapter is to give you an idea of what you can and can't claim for Business Income Tax purposes.

General Definition

Generally, most expenses that a business incurs in producing income are claimable. The best thing that you can do as a business owner is to keep records of everything that you spend that is related to your business. Any expenditure that has a mixed purpose will need to be apportioned between business and private use. Depending on your entity structure, this may be as simple as reducing the claim by the private use or as complicated as lodging a fringe benefits tax return.

Deductions

Let's look at a few of the more common deductions and what you need to think about.

Home-based Businesses

If you work from home, there is the opportunity to claim expenses incurred in the running of your business from home.

All expenses claimed for a home-based business are calculated on an apportionment method. When calculating interest, rates or insurance, these are apportioned on the basis of floor size used.

Example: You use a bedroom in your house as a home office. The floor area of this room is 10m2 and the whole house is 150m2, in this case the business proportion is 10/150 = 6.66%.

These are a few of the major deductions available:

- **Telephone & Internet** – Apportion % on business use.

- **Electricity** – Apportion % on business use or claim ATO Rate based on hours used.

- **Rent** – Apportion on % of floor space used.

- **Insurance** – Apportion on % of floor space used unless specific business equipment listed separately.

- **Rates** – Apportion on % of floor space used.

IT IS IMPORTANT to consider whether the claiming of these expenses may give rise to a capital gain on the sale of your home at a later date. In a strange twist, the ATO does not consider whether or not you actually claimed the expenses on your home, but whether you were entitled to claim, in determining whether or not CGT is payable. Although a bit bizarre, what this really means is that if you work from home, you might as well claim the expenses.

Motor Vehicles

The treatment of motor vehicle expenses differs depending on the type of entity that you operate.

Individual Business Owners and Employees are subject to the same rules. They can claim a business use percentage of their total expenses for the vehicle including interest and depreciation. The reimbursement can be based on either the number of kilometres travelled up to a maximum of 5000km, or if their travel exceeds 5000 km, a percentage of the running costs including depreciation and interest. It is important to ensure that you have records to back up any claim that you make.

Companies and Trusts are precluded from claiming the less than 5000 km "cents per kilometre" method. However, they are able to reimburse individuals that claim should the vehicle be owned by them personally. Any vehicles that are owned by a company and trust will inherently be subject to fringe benefits tax and is essential that adequate logbooks be maintained to determine business and private use.

A Logbook is cheap and is available from most newsagents. The ATO does now recognise electronic forms of recording transactions such as downloadable transactions from a mobile gps device. If you are going to claim a percentage of expenses, it is essential that you maintain all records regarding to the cost of the vehicle. Keep in mind that if you are using a % rate, a logbook needs to be kept for a minimum of 13 consecutive weeks and must record all trips the vehicle undertakes. If you are using the Km method, the logbook must be kept for the full year showing business trips only.

Meal Expenses

We have all heard stories about beer for the boys on Fridays or taking the "Missus" out to lunch and calling it a Directors meeting. The reality is that there are strict rules on meal benefits. These come under the Fringe Benefits Tax rules which were discussed in Chapter 12 – Different Tax Types. It is important to keep expense records whenever you claim any expenses to do with food and drink. Food and drink provided to employees on the premises is generally deductible. Food and drink off premises is generally non-deductible. Xmas parties are non-deductible unless you want to pay FBT at 46.5% on the value which is generally not a good idea. Meals with clients for marketing purposes are deductible for the employee costs but not the expense you incur for your client. You can claim these types of expenses on a 50/50 basis if you have no records as to exactly who was there at the time. So the bottom line here is for every expense you have with meal and drinks, note who was there, where it was and how many employees vs clients, so that you can determine the deductibility of that expense.

Uniforms and Protective Clothing

The cost of purchasing and maintaining uniforms and protective clothing is generally deductible by the employer. In order for uniforms to be deductible, they must either be compulsory or registered on the national uniforms register which has strict rules regarding the number of employees in your business. Uniforms must be easily identifiable as a uniform and not of a general clothing nature; they also must have your logo on them. If you meet these guidelines, then ongoing maintenance and laundry is deductible by your employees too.

Protective clothing needs to be protective. Yes, that sounds obvious but it means they need to be either hi-vis or some kind of rain/dust protection to be claimable. Boots need to be steel capped and generally socks are not deductible. Naturally items like goggles, gloves and hard hats are deductible. A pair of King-Gee shorts is not deductible just because it is classed as work wear, it needs to either be part of a compulsory or registered uniform (with the appropriate logo) or protective in nature. The same goes for blue work shirts. Overalls however are deductible as they are protective.

General Record Retention

All Sales records (invoices & till tapes), Expense invoices and contracts for asset sales and purchases need to be kept for 4 years after your tax lodgement date. This generally creates a nightmare for the business owner. Not only does storing these records become cumbersome the larger your business becomes but some invoices fade and they also present a fire risk. Luckily the ATO has moved into the 21st century and does allow electronic copies of these records, as long as they are easily accessible. This means that if you scan them through to your computer, you need to have another backup somewhere safe should the computer fail.

Cloud-Based storage solutions may be the answer. I'm going to hop on my Xero bandwagon (again) and explain how it works to assist you with this. Xero has a "files" component. You can either email documents to a secure email which stores them directly in your file or you can drag and drop and then browse to find it. Whilst this doesn't sound like anything magical, what you can do with these files once you have them in the system is attach them to transactions in your accounts. This means you can click on the expense in Motor Vehicles and easily find the receipt from BP when you bought your fuel. You could also just save the documents within a folder structure similar to Windows which is a good place to put copies of documents such as insurance policies or staff records.

Xero is not the only solution here. Web-based applications such as www.dropbox.com, www.evernote.com or www.box.com as well as a host of others provide cloud storage of documents. Whilst you can put them there, I think having them attached to the transactions in your accounting system is absolutely legendary (yes that's the accountant coming through!).

Even better than using Xero Files or Dropbox, is a combination of the two with an application that can save you time and effort in your data entry and still give you access to your documents when you want them. We discussed this in Chapter 7 – Bookkeeping and Recordkeeping, using solutions like http://www.receipt-bank.com/ or www.shoeboxed.com together with Xero will give you the best of both worlds.

Tax Returns

Regardless of the entity you operate or whether you make a profit or a loss, Income Tax Returns need to be lodged each year. I recommend the use of a good accountant or tax agent to assist with the preparation of these returns to ensure you have someone double checking what you are claiming to ensure that you claim everything that you are entitled to and that you comply with ATO rules. Another bonus of using a tax agent is that they have concessional lodgement dates so your returns are not due by 31st October.

Individuals and Partnerships – Deferred Losses

If you run your business as a sole trader and make a loss, there are strict rules on whether you are able to claim these losses against other income or whether they need to be deferred. These rules have come in to stop high income earners claiming losses on "hobbies". The good news is that if you make a loss, it can be carried forward indefinitely until you meet the rules to allow it to be claimed. As long as your income from other sources is less than $250,000, if you make a loss and meet one of the following tests then you can claim your losses in the year they were made and also any losses from prior years that have been carried forward:

- Assessable Income – Your business must turnover more than $20,000.

- Profits test – If it has produced a profit in 3 of the past 5 years.

- Real Property Test – Your business uses real property (land & buildings) worth at least $500,000 on a continuing basis.

- Other Assets Test – Your business uses assets worth $100,000 on a continuing basis.

There are special rules if you are operating a primary production business or as an artist. Also there is Commissioner's Discretion in certain circumstances but this is pretty hard to get and a whole lot of paperwork is required to be submitted to the ATO.

This is an area that changes frequently but your tax agent or accountant should know the rules so all I can suggest here is to seek advice if your business is going to make a loss.

Tax Lodgement Dates

Tax Type	Frequency	Due Date
GST	Monthly	21st of next month
GST	Quarterly	28th of next month
PAYGW	Monthly	21st of next month
PAYGW	Quarterly	28th of next month
SGC	Quarterly	28th of next month
Payroll Tax	Monthly	Approx. 7th of next month
FBT	Quarterly	By 21 May each year (1)
Workcover	Annual	Usually by 30 September (2)
Income Tax	Annual	By 31 October each year (3)

(1)   A quarterly instalment then an annual wash-up with lodgement of FBT Return due by 21 May each year.

(2)   Usually by 30 September, some states do allow monthly payments.

(3)   Dependent on your lodgement history and the size of your business. Individuals who lodge themselves need to do so by 31 October each year. If you use a tax agent, then there are different lodgement dates – check with your Accountant.

Tips:

1. Keep all your paperwork, either manually or electronically.

2. Discuss your deductions with your tax agent – it's easier to know the rules up front than risk an audit.

3. Know your lodgement dates.

CHAPTER 14

INTERNAL CHECKS

Internal checks throughout all the business processes is vitally important for the protection of the assets and the effective management of the business. It is all very well to say "I trust my staff" but imagine a situation where all your hard earned cash is lost through human error whether unintentional or otherwise. For example, cash sales are not recorded or an order goes astray because no-one checked the order book? You could also suffer embarrassment from errors in correspondence with your customers or suppliers. The way to minimise the risk of losses is to have basic internal checks whereby the important work of one employee is always checked by another or there are other controls in place that will highlight errors early so that they can be corrected.

Prevention vs. Detection

There are two types of internal checks:

1. Preventative Checks

These are designed to prevent an error occurring. For example:

- Checking supplier's invoices before they are paid.
- Computer password controls.

- Job swapping

Case Study 1: A wages clerk of an engineering company was so conscientious that she seldom took leave and always handled the wages herself. One day she suddenly took ill and was absent for a lengthy period during which time, it was discovered that there were "dummy" employees on the payroll. the company took preventative action by introducing a compulsory leave requirement for all employees.

2. Detective Checks

- Balancing the daily cash takings with till/register tapes.
- Checking that there is an invoice for every delivery.
- Checking the goods delivered to the delivery docket and the delivery docket to the invoice.
- Reviewing Actual Margins to Budgets or costings.

Case Study 2: An international food franchise monitors the average yield from its potato consumption. It came to their attention that the average yield from one of their stores was consistently below the expected levels so they investigated. Guess what? They found that a well-meaning employee was shaking the packets of chips to ensure that they were as full as possible before handing to the customer. This increased the "density" of the chips in the packet which was good for the customer but bad for profits! By establishing and measuring the average content of a packet of chips, the company was able to "detect" the error and take effective action.

Although the examples given relate to large companies, they illustrate the need to have effective internal checks.

"Danger Zones"

Some of the areas to look out for are:

1. Fraud

- Cash sales, particularly where the customer may not require an invoice. If you had a sign stating "no refund without receipt", it would encourage customers to request a receipt, making sure the sale is recorded.

- Unauthorised access to stock that is easily saleable. Keep doors locked and limit access to areas after hours to reduce risk of theft.

- Unauthorised access to computer systems. Ensure all staff have individual passwords that are changed regularly and not shared. Most computer systems have an audit trail but ultimately ensure all confidential documents are password protected.

- One employee is responsible for invoicing, receipting and banking of cash. Where possible have two people responsible for these functions.

- An employee is reluctant to take leave. Having a policy of no accumulation of leave over 4 weeks to deter this action.

2. Errors and Omissions

- One person is responsible for processing orders, invoicing and delivery of goods. Always have a second person sign off to check for errors. Cross-reference totals wherever possible.

- Customer enquiries are not recorded. Set up an enquiry system, this is great for marketing too.

- Unauthorised credit for customers. Limit who can give credit and always do credit checks before authorising credit.

- A disorganised warehouse which could lead to over/under-ordering of supplies. Regular stocktakes will show what needs re-ordering and when. Consider "just-in-time" ordering if it is available at a comparative price. Naturally an organised warehouse will also make production quicker, easier and safer.

"It Starts at The Top"

This may sound like a cliché but it's true. Your staff will judge you on the basis of your personal integrity. It stands to reason that if you are seen to be "bending the rules" or cheating your customers and suppliers, you cannot expect your staff to behave any differently.

CHAPTER 15

XERO AND ITS ECOSYSTEM

Although we spoke about bookkeeping in previous chapters, this chapter on Xero and its Ecosystem is about changing the way that we do things – pushing the boundaries and using technology to its full advantage. We agreed earlier that bookkeeping is booorrring, so let's move away from old desktop processes to the cloud where we can link apps together to let the computers do the majority of the thinking and keep your input to the minimal required.

Cloud technology is something that both HBA Encompass and The Bookkeeper Hub have embraced in full. This allows us, our staff and our clients to be able to work "on the run" and anywhere we have an internet connection. It allows us to work in real time, give relevant advice and help make best of breed decisions. There is no reason why you can't do this too!

Case Study: Imagine having a successful business but juggling this with children playing representative sport. Not only would you need to manage your cash flow and day to day business operations including quotes, delivery, invoicing, wages, account payments but also the demands of being available for your kids as well. By using cloud-based technology, you can do all this with an ipad or phone, anywhere, anytime.

As I have mentioned many times throughout this book, Xero is my accounting or bookkeeping system of choice. Xero Accounting is a cloud-based package, developed by Xero Limited, a company listed on both the New Zealand and Australian stock exchanges and is available worldwide. The thing about Xero software that really "rocks my boat" is the ability to have bank transactions processed on a daily basis. What that actually means is that each night your bank pushes the transactions from your bank account into your accounting package. As a result, all that you need to do is to tell your accounting package what each transaction was for and most of your bookkeeping is done.

All procedures relating to bookkeeping need to be documented. It is essential that there are standard procedures relating to the collation of information, the processing of this information, completing checklists to do with end of month and the end of year requirements, and the actual lodgement of all Tax Office returns. In my day to day occupation as an Accountant I have dealt with a wide range of accounting packages and I can honestly tell you that client feedback is that Xero is by far the easiest bookkeeping system to master. It covers all the areas you expect from a bookkeeping package, banking, Sales, Purchases, Payroll, Budgets and has a massive range of add-ons that make it the ultimate tool for your business.

The Xero add-on marketplace is amazing. There are over 300 cloud based apps or programs that dovetail into the Xero program to advance your business in whichever way you chose – whether it be time saving during the bookkeeping process, following up on debtors, drilling down into the profitability of your business or maintaining an awesome customer relationship. Check out Xero and its add-ons at:

www.xero.com/au

I'm always after ways to simplify and automate my business processes. Below is a list of my favourites and how they can literally save you hours of double input:

Bills and Expenses:

The way these packages/apps work is that you send them a copy or originals of your documentation which they then scan and keep on record for a minimum of 7 years. These applications enable you to code each expense item which is then automatically imported into your Xero accounting software. Generally, once you have coded an expense for a supplier once, it comes up with that automatically going forward, all you need to do is review & export. Within Xero they can be linked directly to a transaction from the bank account, a bill to be paid or an expense to be reimbursed, always allowing you to see the original invoice for each transaction. These apps also pick up the correct GST from the invoice so no splitting is required. The beauty of this is that when you do a bank reconciliation in Xero, bank transactions are automatically linked to these receipts/invoices. If you would like to see a detailed explanation of both of these products, please go to the website and read the blog: www.bookkeeperhub.com.au/blog/Shoeboxed_vs_Receipt_Ba nk

A really useful feature of these apps is the ability to take a photo of bills/receipts with your phone and upload them directly to the system. The really cool thing about this is that it means that you won't accidentally lose those receipts that you file on the floor or your car or in your bulging wallet. No more snap-lock bags to keep all your receipts, no receipts fading, just a simple way of recording them and being able to allocate the expense at a later date.

My favourites (in order):

- Receiptbank: http://www.receipt-bank.com/

  It takes all your invoices and converts them into bills to be paid in Xero. It not only automatically codes the expenses but also attaches a PDF copy to each bill in case you need to refer to it later.

- Shoeboxed: www.shoeboxed.com.au

  Like Receiptbank it takes all your invoices and converts them to bills but it also has the ability to mail paper bills to Shoeboxed for processing and get them back to store yourself, although I'm not sure why anyone would want to get them back! PDF copies are stored in Shoeboxed with a link back to Xero rather than stored in Xero itself.

Currently Receiptbank is my preference as it is the easiest interface to use. It does however depend on what features you want as they are all slightly different.

Debtor Tracking:

These apps link to your Xero to send reminders to your customers regarding accounts payable. What is important to me is customisation – the ability to customise your emails or texts that go out to clients to remind them that a bill is due. Most of them start with a reminder that your bill is due in a few days, followed up by a reminder that it is due today, due last week etc. and they process gets heavier until ultimately a debt collection process is started. Hopefully it won't come to that, evidence quoted by Chaser (discussed below) is that on average their clients get paid 26 days earlier than before using Chaser.

My favourites (in order):

- Chaser: www.chaser.com.au

    Chaser not only allows you to fully customise the timing of your reminders but also allows you to halt chasing on individual invoices or all invoices for individual clients. Another great feature is that if a customer owes you several invoices, it receives one reminder of what is due rather than one for each invoice which really reeks of automation.

- Debtor Daddy: www.debtordaddy.com

  The original Debtor Tracking App which has undergone massive refurbishment in the last 18 months. It is tried and tested.

- SMS my Debtors: www.smsmydebtors.com

  SMS my Debtors does what it says, instead of using emails to chase debtors it sends them SMS Reminders.

- Iodm: www.iodm.com.au

  Iodm uses a combination of Letters and SMS alerts leading up to final demands and automatic referral to a debt collection company.

- Vision6: www.vision6.com.au

  Vision6 is more than a debt collection app, it is a smart email and SMS marketing app which is why I've included it here. So much more yet prices start at only $9 per month. I haven't used it so cannot comment on ease of setup.

- Xero: www.xero.com/au

  Xero has not introduced a debtor reminder system but I don't believe it is as intuitive as the others and will chase each invoice separately.

To date I haven't used any of these products personally, we are currently looking at them for our own use and that of our clients so it's best to check them all out and make your own decision. These ones listed are here because I have seen them demonstrated or heard about them on industry podcasts.

Ecommerce

If you are going to have an online store, then having an ecommerce app that links with Xero is essential. TradeGecko is my choice here because not only does it link seamlessly with your ecommerce but also manages your inventory.

Inventory

Xero has just upgraded its inventory function but if you have a big range of products or want to drill down in detail on individual products, I suggest you look at an inventory app. Unleashed is the most well used, probably due to it being one of the original add-on apps. TradeGecko also features here.

Point of Sale

Online point of sale software is a must for all retail businesses. Vend not only manages inventory but also records the sales process. Cin7 seems to have more features including inventory, point of sale, warehouse management and wholesale features. Ultimately it comes down to which features you need and making sure that they fit exactly to your business.

Payments

Imagine a world where you can put a link on your invoice so that customers can pay you directly as soon as they see the invoice or reminder. This world is here. The integration is easy and reconciliation of payments automatically links back to each bulk deposit. Naturally all these solutions come with corresponding Merchant Fees so you need to weigh up the negative impact of these fees on your cash flow.

My favourites (in order)

- IntegraPay: www.integrapay.com.au

  IntegraPay is simple to use and can be setup in under 24 hours. IntegraPay's merchant fees are extremely competitive and it not only accepts credit card but can do recurring direct debits straight from invoice terms.

- Eway: www.eway.com.au

  Eway is simple and easy to use, their customer service is awesome and it they state you can get up and running in 4 days. Credit Card payments in real time is great for your cash flow.

- Stripe: www.stripe.com

  Stripe is easy to use and reasonably cost effective but does take up to 7 days for the funds to come in.

Payroll

Xero itself has an adequate payroll system but if you have multiple shifts and awards or lots of employees, it would be easier and cheaper to use a payroll add-on to simplify the data entry. Automatic entry of timesheets by staff on different sites and rostering is another reason to use a payroll add-on.

My favourites (in order):

- Deputy: www.deputy.com.au

  Deputy not only manages rosters and timesheets but it also incorporates award rates, fatigue management and KPI management. It is completely cloud based with iphone, android and ipad apps to allow for login on or off-site.

- Tanda: www.tanda.com.au

  Tanda not only does rostering and awards but it also has its own dedicated time clock system.

Human Resources Management

If you have staff, you need a system to record their hiring, manage interactions and terminations. Assistance from an HR Consultant or Lawyer can be extremely expensive yet save you thousands of dollars should any HR component be mismanaged. Enable HR http://www.enablehr.com.au and Employment Hero assist not only with the management of your resources but also contracts, policies, performance management & Workplace Health & Safety Obligations. They automatically take the base employment details directly from Xero.

Regardless of which add-ons you choose, it's important to look at all available and choose those that fit your needs exactly. There are integrators out there who specialise in different industries and lots of bookkeepers and accountants who have knowledge of many of the add-ons.

Although I constantly mention how easy Xero is to use, a range of tutorials for Xero are available both on the Xero website www.Xero.com/au and on The Bookkeeper Hub website www.bookkeeperhub.com.au

If it all sounds a bit overwhelming, The Bookkeeper Hub can not only provide training and assistance with integration but it also has bookkeeping services to actually process all your bookkeeping and payroll needs.

To Do:

1. Review the actions in your business that can be automated.

2. Review the add-ons and choose based on best fit.

3. Consider if you want to do it yourself or outsource to The Bookkeeper Hub.

CHAPTER 16

HOW TO MANAGE IT ALL

Are you overwhelmed yet? We have covered a lot of things in this book, some of which will seem like common sense and some of it is downright scary. When starting a business there are so many things to think about and to keep track of everything sometimes seems insurmountable. Here are a few ideas to help you manage it and not lose your mind!

Daily Goal and Task Setting

One of the best ways that I know of to work out where I need to be at the end of the day is to set my daily goals. I look at the tasks that need to be completed, prioritise these into order by urgency, and then determine how many of these I expect to get done today. This gives me a list that I can check off and feel some sense of achievement. You will also find that your life is a lot better organised and less stressful. Having said that, don't be surprised if you sometimes get to the end of the day and find that you have not dealt with anything on your list – there will always be the unexpected!

This daily goal setting can be extended to weekly, monthly and yearly goals and related tasks. This was covered in some detail in the planning section but a "One Page" Plan to remind you where you want to be, broken down into small action tasks will keep you on the path you want to follow. Naturally if you change path, you will need to change plans.

Daily Huddle (10 to 10)

If you have staff involved in your business, it's important to include them in the daily goal and task setting. In our business we have what is called a "10 to 10" meeting. This is a quick meeting of our staff where we list what each of us is going to do for the day, and if there is anything that will stop us from getting it done. The idea is to go around the group from person to person first going through what each of us will be doing today and listing how we will know that we have achieved the goals. We then go round again to see if anybody is "stuck". This ensures that everyone knows what everybody else is doing, and highlights anyone who is overloaded and needs assistance. If anyone is "stuck", due to a lack of information or unavailability of a colleague, this can be sorted out there and then so that they are able to fulfil their daily goals. It also makes people realise that other people are busy even though they may not seem so.

An example of a daily task list and 10 to 10 format template can be found at www.yourvirtualcfo.com/templates/daily. It is a good idea to laminate the blank templates and write on them with erasable markers. This enables you to wipe them clean and re-use them without consuming reams and reams of paper.

Automation

Automate where possible. The idea here is merely to work smarter rather than harder. Depending on your business there may be numerous "cloud based" packages or programs that can really assist you in cutting down on the number of things you need to do in your day. It is essential to make sure that where possible, your computer programs talk to one another. There is no benefit in having an awesome Customer Relations Management (CRM) system if every time you update an address, you then need to go and change it in your accounting system to invoice the client. It is also essential in making sure all that all processes and procedures and documents are easily available to the people that need them.

Useful Cloud Apps

A range of products that I find extremely useful in running a business and that can be automated together are as follows (check our website for updates to this list as technology continually changes)

- Bookkeeping – Xero

- Receipt Storage & Entry into Xero – Shoeboxed or Receipt Bank

- Workflow Scheduling – WorkflowMax & Basecamp

- Debtor Collection – Debtor Daddy

- Data Storage – Dropbox, Google Drive, Evernote, Box.com

- Document Creation – Google Docs, Office 365 (think Mail, Word, Excel)

- Marketing – Mailchimp & Survey Monkey

- Lead Management – WorkflowMax

- Event management – Eventbright

- Event Hosting – GoToWebinar

- Customer Service – Zendesk

- Connecting it all together – Zapier

This looks like a very long list, but the important thing here is to get it to work for you. Imagine entering a customer on a CRM system, which automatically creates a job in your job management software, a prospective client in your accounting software, and a contact in your marketing software. All of this with one simple entry that connects and automates over 250 web apps. In my mind perhaps Zapier (or something like it) is one of the most important applications here because it really links everything together to eliminate double or triple data entry.

Do keep in mind however, that all of these apps do charge on a monthly basis and just because something is "cool or groovy", you may not necessarily need it in your business at this time. All these monthly subscriptions do add up.

Delegation

Letting go is one of the hardest things for business owners to do. Every process or procedure that you go through during your day needs to be looked at to see if there can be savings in your time by outsourcing or handing down jobs where possible. Outsourcing does not necessarily have to mean a staff member sitting in India or the Philippines, it can be as simple as getting an external resource like a contracted administration clerk to take the day-to-day administrative work off your hands or a marketing consultant to schedule your Facebook marketing.

You always need to keep in mind that while cash flow may be tight, you need to be performing a role in your business that is going to generate the most value. Believe it, the ideal solution is a combination of outsourcing and automation. A perfect example of this was mentioned when we talked about bookkeeping in Chapter 7 – the use of programs such as Receipt Bank will cut down the bookkeeping time required because it dovetails in with Xero.

Mentors and Coaches

Another way to try to keep on top of everything is to seek advice from people who have "been there and done that".

Mentors

Mentors are generally a non-paid position. What this basically means is that you seek out a person who has experience in an area of your business that you need assistance with. This person may or may not be in the industry you are involved in. For instance, if you know that you weak at marketing, it would be wise to find a mentor that has had considerable experience in marketing, even if they are not in your industry.

Mentors are usually happy to provide their advice for free but here's an interesting thought – whilst your finances may be limited, using a paid mentor may be a better use of resources. It sounds strange that you would want to pay someone when you could possibly get someone to assist you for free, but the logic behind this is that the paid mentor will have more time for you if he/she is being remunerated for their time. You will also make better use of your time by using the mentor to make sure that you are getting the answers that you need, and not waffling on. Think of it like this, if you had a paid mentor, you would not pay for him or her to come and have a general chat. You're more likely to prepare yourself in advance of when they are coming, have a list of the questions and ideas that you want to bounce off them and make the best of the time you have available.

Business Coaches

Are mentors and business coaches the same? The answer is no. A mentor is generally someone you can bounce ideas off, get feedback, and use their wealth of experience to come up with a decision yourself. A coach will generally assist you with the fundamentals of running your business. A coach may assist you with processes and procedures and keep you accountable for what happens within your business. Think of a coach as a football coach for your business and a mentor being a manager looking after the players, pointing them in the right direction on their journey.

The bottom line is, it's good to talk to people who are more experienced, whether they are mentors or other people in your industry. These people are able to give you feedback on the things that you are doing well, the things that you are not doing well and areas that may or may not have worked for them in the past so that you don't make the same mistakes!

Plan and Measure Performance

There cannot be enough emphasis on the need for planning and measuring performance for both the business and the people in it. Without a clear plan of where you want to go and how you intend getting there will result in one of two things:

1. Enormous frustration and financial loss in the medium to long term.

2. Failure to realise the full potential of your business.

Set clear measurable goals and assess your performance on a regular basis and you will go a long way towards achieving your dreams.

Tips:

1. **Set daily, Weekly & Monthly Goals.**

2. **Daily Huddle**

3. **Automate where possible.**

4. **Find good Mentors and use them wisely.**

GLOSSARY

ABN – Australian Business Number

ARIA – Australian Recording Industry Association

ASIC – Australian Securities Investment Commission

ATO – Australian Taxation Office

BAS – Business Activity Statement (GST Return)

BAS Agent – Registered Agent (Usually Bookkeeper) who can prepare Business Activity Statements and provide GST advice

CGT – Capital Gains Tax

FBT – Fringe Benefits Tax

GST – Goods & Services Tax

HR – Human Resources

IAS – Instalment Activity Statement (PAYG Withholding or Instalment Return)

IP – Intellectual Property

PAYG – Pay as You Go Tax – ether withholding for Staff or Instalments for companies & sole traders

PAYG Summary – Yearly summary of wages earned (old Group Certificate)

PI – Professional Indemnity

QBCC – Queensland Building & Construction Commission

SEO – Search Engine Optimisation

SGC – Superannuation Guarantee Charge

SWOT Analysis – Strengths, Weaknesses, Opportunities, Strengths

Tax Agent – Accountant registered with ATO to prepare tax returns and give tax advice

TFN – Tax File Number

UCP – Unique Champions Position (Similar to USP)

USP – Unique Service Position

WIP – Work In Process

USEFUL WEBSITE LINKS

Chapter 1 – Planning

Vern Harnish One Page Plan:
www.gazelles.com

Australian Government Business:
www.business.gov.au

Chapter 2 –Marketing

Document Management for downloads

Box:
www.box.com

Dropbox:
www.dropbox.com

Evernote:
www.evernote.com

Google Docs:
https://www.google.com/docs/about/

Office365:
https://products.office.com/en-au/home

Social Media Management

Aweber:
www.aweber.com

Bitly:
www.bitly.com

Buffer:
www.buffer.com

Crowdbooster:
www.crowdbooster.com

Everypost:
http://everypost.me/

Facebook:
www.facebook.com

Google+:
https://plus.google.com

Hootsuite:
www.hootsuite.com

Instagram:
www.instagram.com

LinkedIn:
www.linkedin.com

Social Flow:
www.socialflow.com

Social Oomph:
www.socialoomph.com

Sprout Social:
www.sproutsocial.com

Tweepi:
www.tweepi.com

Twitter:
www.twitter.com

Campaigns

Campaign Monitor:
www.campaignmonitor.com

Leadpages:
www.leadpages.net

MailChimp:
www.mailchimp.com

Survey Monkey:
www.surveymonkey.com

Vision6:
www.vision6.com.au

Outsourcing

Fiverr:
www.fiverr.com

Upwork:
www.upwork.com

Events

GotoMeeting:
www.gotomeeting.com.au

Eventbright:
www.eventbright.com.au

Skype:
www.skype.com

App Linking

Zapier:
www.zapier.com

Customer Service

Zendesk:
www.zendesk.com

Chapter 3 – Business Structures

ASIC:
www.asic.gov.au

Chapter 4 – Licencing

ASIC:
www.asic.gov.au

Fairwork Australia:
www.fairwork.gov.au

Geoff Moller (Trademarks):
www.geoffmoller.com

IP Australia (Trademarks):
www.ipaustralia.gov.au

Queensland Building & Construction Commission (QBCC):
www.qbcc.qld.gov.au

Chapter 5 – Processes & Procedures

Basecamp:
www.basecamp.com

Google Docs:
https://www.google.com/docs/about/

GotoMeeting:
www.gotomeeting.com.au

Office365:
https://products.office.com/en-au/home

Skype:
www.skype.com

Chapter 6 – Bookkeeping

Bookkeeping

The Bookkeeper Hub:
www.bookkeeperhub.com.au

HBA Encompass:
www.hbaencompass.com.au

Receipt Bank:
http://www.receipt-bank.com/

Shoeboxed:
www.shoeboxed.com

Xero:
www.xero.com/au

Document Management

Box:
www.box.com

Dropbox:
www.dropbox.com

Evernote:
www.evernote.com

Google Docs:
https://www.google.com/docs/about/

Office365:
https://products.office.com/en-au/home

Payment Gateways

Eway:
www.eway.com.au

PayPal:
www.paypal.com

Stripe:
www.stripe.com

Payroll & Staff Management

Deputy:
www.deputy.com

Tanda:
www.tanda.co

Inventory & Point of Sale

TradeGecko:
www.tradegecko.com

Unleashed:
www.unleashedsoftware.com

Vend:
www.vendhq.com

Workflow Management

WorkflowMax:
www.workflowmax.com

Additional Xero Add-Ons:
https://www.xero.com/au/add-ons/

Chapter 8 – Cash Flow Management

Debtor Collection

Chaser:
www.chaser.com

Debtor Daddy:
www.debtordaddy.com

Iodm:
www.iodm.com.au

SMS My Debtors:
www.smsmydebtors.com

Chapter 10 – Staff

Australian Government:
www.business.gov.au

Employee vs Contractor tools:
https://www.ato.gov.au/Calculators-and-tools/Building-and-construction-industry---employee/contractor-decision-tool/

Deputy:
www.deputy.com

Employment Hero:
www.employmenthero.com.au

Fairwork Australia:
www.fairwork.gov.au

Enable HR:
www.enablehr.com.au

Superannuation – Ordinary Times Earnings:
https://www.ato.gov.au/Business/Employers-super/How-much-to-pay-and-when-to-pay/Ordinary-time-earnings/Checklist-for-salary-or-wages-and-ordinary-time-earnings/

Super Stream:
https://www.youtube.com/watch?v=sB3CWx0Zhho

Chapter 12 – Different Tax Types

Australian Taxation Office (ATO):
www.ato.gov.au

ATO – New Business Registrations:
https://www.ato.gov.au/business/registration/register-your-new-business/

ATO – PAYG Withholding Tables:
https://www.ato.gov.au/rates/tax-tables/

ATO – Small Business Superannuation Clearing House:
https://www.ato.gov.au/Business/Employers-super/In-detail/Small-Business-Superannuation-Clearing-House/Using-the-small-business-superannuation-clearing-house/

GST Food Classifications:
www.ato.gov.au/Business/Consultation--Business/In-detail/Food-industry/Food-classification-for-GST/GST-food-guide/

GST Free Items:
https://www.ato.gov.au/Business/GST/When-to-charge-GST-(and-when-not-to)/GST-free-sales

Superannuation – Ordinary Times Earnings:
https://www.ato.gov.au/Business/Employers-super/How-much-to-pay-and-when-to-pay/Ordinary-time-earnings/Checklist-for-salary-or-wages-and-ordinary-time-earnings/

Super Stream:
https://www.youtube.com/watch?v=sB3CWx0Zhho

Chapter 15 – Xero and its Ecosystem

Bookkeeping

Receipt Bank:
http://www.receipt-bank.com

Shoeboxed:
www.shoeboxed.com

Xero:
www.xero.com/au

Document Management

Box:
www.box.com

Dropbox:
www.dropbox.com

Evernote:
www.evernote.com

Google Docs:
https://www.google.com/docs/about/

Office365:
https://products.office.com/en-au/home

Payment Gateways

Eway:
www.eway.com.au

PayPal:
www.paypal.com

Stripe:
www.stripe.com

Payroll & Staff Management

Deputy:
www.deputy.com

Tanda:
www.tanda.co

Inventory & Point of Sale

TradeGecko:
www.tradegecko.com

Unleashed:
www.unleashedsoftware.com

Vend:
www.vendhq.com

Workflow Management

WorkflowMax:
www.workflowmax.com

Additional Xero Add-Ons:
https://www.xero.com/au/add-ons/

General Useful Websites

www.business.gov.au

www.xero.com/au/startups/

State Small Businesses:
www.business.vic.gov.au (replace your "vic" with your state)